THE WRIGHT SPACE

THE WRIGHT SPACE

▼ Spencer Hart ▼

Barnes
& Noble
Books

NEW YORK

This 2007 edition published by Barnes and Noble, Inc. by arrangement with Saraband

Photography: Balthazar Korab, Paul Rocheleau
(for detailed credits and supplementary photographer credits, please see page 256)
Book design: Nikki L. Fesak
Cover design: Erin Pikor

ISBN 13: 978-0-7607-7450-2
ISBN-10: 0-7607-7450-1

Library of Congress Cataloging in Publication Data available

Printed and bound in China

3 5 7 9 10 8 6 4 2

Page 1: *The striking geometry of the coffered skylights illuminating the Unity Temple in Oak Park, Illinois, exemplifies the blend of simplicity, beauty, and practicality unique to Wright's designs.*

Page 2: *The bedroom/study at Taliesin, Spring Green, Wisconsin, which has been described as Wright's "autobiography in wood and stone."*

THIS BOOK IS DEDICATED
TO THE MEMORY OF
MARGARET BELL HART

Contents

INTRODUCTION

American architect Frank Lloyd Wright (1867–1959) has been called the greatest single influence on twentieth-century design. His seventy-year career spanned an era of enormous change in the nation and the world, and he was in the vanguard of those who sought to make architecture relevant to the social and cultural dynamic of their time. Reluctant to acknowledge outside influences on his own remarkable work, he gave credit to only a few, including his mentor the American architect Louis Sullivan (1856–1924), with whom he worked for five years in Chicago; the Japanese aesthetic reflected in his extensive collection of wood-block prints; and the British Arts and Crafts movement, which he was instrumental in introducing to the United States.

By turns autocratic and charming, Wright inspired strong feelings—pro and con— in those who worked closely with him, from family members to employees, colleagues, students, and clients. His often tempestuous relationships, however, are not the subject of this book, which seeks to identify his unique contribution to architecture and the decorative arts, which he merged in the concept he described as "organic architecture." He was essentially an artist, and his work combined two types of design that had long been defined as separate entities: two-dimensional designs made for flat surfaces and including drawing, painting, and the creation of patterns on fabrics, glass, and wall coverings; and three-dimensional designs including architecture, sculpture, furniture, fixtures, and pottery. All of these elements figured in his work during the several stages of his career, creatively combined to make "the Wright space" an unmistakable environment whose unity was based upon the free-flowing

forms seen in nature, from the spiraling structure of seashells to the arrangement of petals on a flower. Only recently has science discovered that these forms, once believed to be random, are governed by the laws of geometry, calculus, and other branches of pure mathematics. From boyhood, Wright seemed to have an intuitive knowledge of the patterns in natural relationships, perhaps strengthened by what he called "the Froebel gifts"—wooden geometric forms designed by the German educator Friedrich Froebel in the 1830s to teach children elements of structure, mathematics, and creative design. Years afterward, Wright recalled that "the maple-wood blocks…all are in my fingers to this day."

A recurring motif in his designs was the Tree of Life, rendered in art glass, textiles, and decorative geometric lamps like those designed for his second home/studio, Taliesin, in Spring Green, Wisconsin. Several of his buildings spring from this theme, including the Price Tower (1952) in Bartlesville, Oklahoma, which originated in an unrealized project from 1929 for New York City's historic church St. Mark's-in-the-Bowerie. Wright himself described the innovative Price building in *The Story of the Tower* (Horizon Press, 1956): "This skyscraper, planned to stand free in an open park and thus be more fit for human occupancy, is as nearly organic as steel in tension and concrete in compression can make it…Each floor proceeds outward from the [central] shaft as a cantilever slab…similar to the branch of a tree from its trunk." This striking multiuse structure was completed only six years before the architect's death in 1959.

New materials and techniques in architecture evolved rapidly during the nineteenth century, and Wright was always

Page 6: Detail of the entry to Wright's Studio at Oak Park, where he opened his own practice adjacent to his home in 1898.

alert to the chance of testing their capabilities—sometimes to their limit. The Romans had been the first to build with concrete, which provided the massive curving walls they required to provide great public buildings like marketplaces, baths, and the Colosseum, which gave rise to the expression "bread and circuses" as a means of maintaining civil order. Wright experimented with poured concrete as early as 1904, when his Unitarian congregation in Oak Park, Illinois, commissioned him to build a new house of worship. His Unity Temple bore little resemblance to the Gothic Revival church that had preceded it. In his text for the Wasmuth portfolio of his early works, published in Germany in 1910, Wright described the building as "a concrete monolith cast in wooden forms. After removal of forms, exterior surfaces washed clean to expose the small gravel aggregate, the finished result not unlike a coarse granite." Exterior columns and ornaments were of the same material. The interior represented an entirely new kind of space for communal use, with its weight-bearing volumes cleanly defined by the slender wooden uprights; natural lighting through ribbons of second-story windows and coffered amber skylights; and a projecting podium that served to unify speaker and audience.

Other early essays in concrete included the landmark Aline Barnsdall House (1917) located in Los Angeles, California, often called Hollyhock House for its stylized floral motifs. Originally intended as another poured-concrete structure on the grand scale, its construction materials were changed to wood frame and cement plaster except for the identifying hollyhock ornaments and finials. Wright's interest in pre-Columbian design is apparent in the massive closed volumes of the house, which has few windows and no view of its site except from the terraces and rooftops.

The 1920s saw four additional houses in California, which were built in what Wright called his textile-block system, which was a series of concrete blocks impressed with decorative patterns in molds, then "woven together" with steel rods concealed in their hollow grooves. Both floral and geometric designs were employed. The richly embellished blocks were laid up in columns to

Below: *The nineteen-story Harold C. Price Company Tower in Bartlesville, Oklahoma (1952), is cantilevered from a single concrete shaft that rises through the building like a tree trunk to support the "branches."*

create imposing interiors that gave one the sense of living within a sculpture. Other experiments in concrete-block and poured-concrete construction include New York City's renowned Solomon R. Guggenheim Museum (under development from 1943 until 1956) and Wright's last residential design, the Norman Lykes House (1959), which was not constructed until 1967, in Phoenix, Arizona. As architectural writer Fred A. Bernstein described it after its 1990s restoration by Linda Melton and Dallas designer Mil Bodron (*Metropolitan Home*, Nov/Dec 1997): "Like Wright's most famous house, Pennsylvania's Fallingwater, Melton's dwelling treads lightly on its site. Amazingly, its supple forms are made entirely of rectangular concrete blocks. In Wright's hands, the blocks form a sculpture that is organic, nurturing and womblike."

Wright was equally adept in other types of masonry, including brick and stone, and had a deep affinity for fine wood in mellow tones, which he used to define the planes of the horizontal Prairie Houses that first brought him to national and international prominence. Their low-lying roofs and wide eaves seemed to hover over the house, contributing to the sense of shelter and privacy. His fenestration brought windows from the realm of glass holes in walls to a high form of decorative art, set in long bands or ribbons, often high in the wall, and subtly colored to bring out their stylized motifs, including prairie sumac and other plants native to the Midwest. His interiors show a masterful use of oak, mahogany, cypress, cherry, and other woods in the form of bands or stringcourses used to define spatial volumes,

Below: Angled seating with built-in tables and shelving focuses the living room of the Peter A. Beachy House in Oak Park (1906) on the handsome brick fireplace banded with stonework.

along with built-in and freestanding furniture, screening, spindles, and other elements of his own design. Many clients gave him a free hand in every aspect of their commissions, although he was notorious for exceeding budgets and took a proprietary interest in every structure he built—to the extent of moving (or removing) objects that he found incongruent with his overall plan. Utilitarian features like radiators and window screens were offensive to his eye, and if he couldn't conceal them in an artful manner he might arbitrarily dismiss them. (One unfortunate family suffered clouds of mosquitos every summer for years because Wright felt that screening marred his windows.)

One of Wright's earliest objectives was to "break out of the box," as he described traditional architecture, and to devise informal floor plans in which the rooms extended outward from a central core—usually a fireplace in the principal common space—allowing each room or living area to receive light from three different directions. Flexible screening and furniture arrangements served to define the various functions of communal areas like living and dining rooms, while the bedrooms often occupied a wing or floor of their own to provide maximum privacy. Much of his early work under the aegis of Adler & Sullivan (1888–93) involved the remodeling of typical late nineteenth-century houses in Oak Park and other affluent suburbs of Chicago. (He also "bootlegged" some commissions on his own, which led to his rupture with Louis Sullivan and the establishment of his own practice.) Never reticent in expressing his opinions, Wright was typically outspoken in his criticism of the reigning residential styles, including Queen Anne, Gothic,

Tudor Revival, and neo-Colonial. In his book *Drawings and Plans of Frank Lloyd Wright: The Early Period (1893–1909),* he stated that "Our better-class residences are chiefly tributes to English architecture, cut open inside and embellished to suit; porches and 'conveniences' added: the result in most cases, a pitiful mongrel."

After his marriage to Catherine Tobin in his early twenties, and the rapid growth of their family to six children, Wright used his own Oak Park home at 351 Chicago Avenue as a template for his burgeoning ideas on an architecture in which form not only followed function, as Louis Sullivan had asserted, but became one with it. Between 1885 and 1897, this Shingle-style house with its high triangular gable was extended and changed repeatedly, gaining a new dining room (with the innovation of overhead recessed lighting); a barrel-vaulted upstairs playroom; an octagonal bay on the north wall of the living room; and eventually, a separate studio connected to the house by a passageway. Here, Wright's creativity had free reign, as seen in the studio's elegant skylighted reception room, octagonal library, and two-story drafting room lighted by clerestory windows, with a balcony suspended partly by heavy metal chains. In 1906 the studio was reconfigured to provide a direct entrance from Chicago Avenue by way of a terrace leading to a narrow portico. Two sets of low brick piers topped by pedestaled urns flanked the double entry stairs to the terrace, which bore plaques emblematic of the architect's profession and a powerful sculpture created by Richard Bock, who worked on many Wright commissions at this time. The compression of space in and around the entry was designed to heighten the sense of expectation about the building's

Above: Textile-block arcades frame the imposing multilevel interior of the Ennis-Brown House in Los Angeles (1923).

interior—a plan that the architect would use repeatedly throughout his career. Wright historian William Allin Storrer has observed astutely that "A room to Frank Lloyd Wright was space, not the walls surrounding the space, but 'the space within to be lived in,' as Wright quoted Lao Tse" (*The Frank Lloyd Wright Companion*, University of Chicago Press, 1993).

Wright's ideas first came to national attention in 1901, when he published several of his Prairie House-style plans in *The Ladies' Home Journal*. The first was entitled "A Home in a Prairie Town," for which working drawings could be purchased by *Journal* readers from the Curtis Publishing Company. The rendering, in Wright's

inimitable draftsmanship, showed a handsome horizontal house that faced the street and had two tiers of shallow, broad-eaved hipped roofs and bands of casement windows on both levels. The recessed entryway was framed by a Romanesque arch in the style popularized by the American architect Henry Hobson Richardson (1838–86), whose work Wright admired. Richardson, in turn, had trained a generation of architects including Charles McKim, George Shepley, and Stanford White. Though he schooled in Classicism at the Parisian *École des Beaux Arts*, Richardson developed a unique style of his own that led many scholars to rank him as the greatest architect of his time.

Wright's second design for *The Ladies' Home Journal*, "A Small House with Lots of Room in It," was closely approximated by the E. Arthur Davenport House of 1901 in River Forest, Illinois, built in collaboration with Webster Tomlinson. This was a two-story structure of stained-wood board and batten with plaster surfacing below the gabled roofline. It had continuous bands of windows and a terrace (removed at a later date). As with most of the Prairie Houses, both attic and basement were eliminated (a feature of his later Usonian houses of the 1930s and '40s, when live-in servants had almost disappeared from the domestic scene).

Wright's first independent commission was for the William H. Winslow House (1893), also built in River Forest. Its design elements prefigured hallmarks of the Wright style that would be reprised for decades to come. The low foundation of white cast stone ties the house to its site, like the continuous base, or stylobate, that anchored a row of columns in Greco-Roman architecture. Mellow tapestry brick surfaces the first floor, while the narrower second-floor façade is treated as a gallery, faced with an overall foliage pattern in gypsum inspired by the work of Louis Sullivan. The hipped roof has broad, sheltering eaves and is crowned with a low massive chimney of brick and stone. Wright's client was a close friend, and the two produced notable handmade books in the Arts and Crafts style in the three-story stable adjoining the house, which doubled as the Auvergne Press, where Winslow pursued his hobby. Their best-known publication was written by William C. Gannet and designed and decorated by Wright. It was entitled, appropriately, *The House Beautiful*. The volume is now a valuable collector's item, and the Winslow House and Stable are among the seventeen structures by Frank Lloyd Wright that have been designated for preservation by the American Institute of Architects.

The Winslow House was such a major step forward in residential design that Wright made it the subject of the 1931 Kahn Lectures at Princeton University, published as *Modern Architecture* that same year by the Princeton University Press. As he explained it: "The rooms above come through in a continuous window series, under the broad eaves of a gently sloping over-hanging roof. This made enclosing screens out of the lower walls as well as light screens out of the second-story walls. Here was true enclosure of interior space."

Examples of Wright's work published in the Wasmuth portfolio and international design magazines seized the imagination of many young European architects and engineers in the years before World War I. Four of these would make major contributions to Modern architecture: Walter Gropius, Mies van der Rohe, J.J.P. Oud, and the Swiss-born Charles-Edouard Jeanneret, better known as Le Corbusier, who worked in France from 1922. They agreed that most European architecture was not designed for its purpose: based upon ancient styles, it failed to meet the needs of twentieth-century life. However, many of their experiments were at variance with the vision of Frank Lloyd Wright. They turned to steel and concrete skeletons that made heavy masonry walls unnecessary and used glass curtain walls to admit natural daylight, striving to eliminate ornament and to make their stark buildings "machines for living." What became described as the International Style was roundly criticized by Wright, who gave a scathing lecture on "The Cardboard House" at Princeton University in 1930. In *Architecture of the 20th Century* (Brompton Books, 1988), Mary Hollingsworth sums up Wright's opinions on the impersonality of the International Style: "Starting with the anthropomorphic view of the house, likening electric wiring to the nervous system and plumbing to the digestive system, he criticized modern architecture on the grounds that it did not take the organic nature of architecture into consideration, but sought to impose universal solutions."

A decade later, all of Wright's buildings were based on such geometric forms as the triangle and the arc, and his final works repeated the motifs of the spiral, circle, and hexagon, but none of these structures could be described as cold or impersonal. They were always tailored to the needs of his clients and the nature of their sites—eminently livable and designed to grow and change with the circumstances of the families or organizations that they housed. Their inspiration derived from the extensive model called Broadacre City, created by Wright and his associates in the Taliesin Fellowship established at his Wisconsin home/studio in the early 1930s. Broadacre City's Utopian premise called for decentralized urban planning, spacious parklike surroundings, and affordable, modern homes described as Usonian (an acronym for the United States of North America). The 12-foot square (3.7-meter) model was constructed for the 1935 Industrial Arts Exhibition at New York City's Rockefeller Center, where it attracted great attention. The first Usonian house was built the following year for Herbert and Katherine Jacobs of Madison, Wisconsin, who did much of the work themselves to keep costs

moderate. (The home cost some $5,500 when it was built during the Depression.)

The prototype Usonian incorporated new features appropriate to the changes that had taken place in American society since Wright began his career in the late 1900s. It was set upon a concrete slab in which heating coils were embedded in gravel, obviating the need for a basement. Brick wall masses carried most of the supports for the flat roof, and the remaining walls were of prefabricated wood and insulated plywood. Glass doors and bands of clerestory windows provided ample natural light. The street side of the house was almost featureless: it faced inward toward the sloping garden at the rear. From this time onward, many of Wright's designs maximized privacy in similar ways, whether through indoor garden rooms that flowed visually into the outdoor space, or sheltered courtyards nearly enclosed by the dwelling, as in Hispanic building styles. During his early period, when houses and grounds were generally larger, he had designed extensive terraces, balconies, and plantings for his clients: unfortunately, most of these have been obliterated by subdivision of the original properties, razing of the structures themselves, or the high cost of grounds maintenance beginning after World War I.

A notable landscape design was provided by Wright's associate Walter Burley Griffin for the William E. Martin House (1902) in Oak Park. Its large level lot at 636 North East Avenue allowed for an impressive three-story house with long wings at ground-floor level and windows that extended around the corners of the house. A wooden pergola was joined to one of the porches, with gardens on either side, and the property was enhanced by pools, bridges, and a lawn tennis court. Martin's enthusiasm for Wright's work was communicated to his brother Darwin D. Martin, a Buffalo, New York, businessman, who commissioned two new houses: an extremely large Prairie-style house located in Buffalo (1904) with a 100-foot-long (30-meter) glass-enclosed pergola, and, much later, the country house called Graycliff (1927), in Derby, New York. Its site was a high bluff overlooking Lake Erie, and the interior centered on the chimney core formed of rugged fieldstone. Multilevel hipped and gabled rooflines beneath towering trees gave it the air of a hunting lodge.

Wherever possible, Wright incorporated native materials into his designs, as seen in the limestone walls and courtyards of Taliesin in Spring Green, and the multicolored desert-rubblestone foundations and exterior paving at his Taliesin West in Scottsdale, Arizona. By the same token, he preserved and highlighted regional plant materials, from the native shrubs and wayside flowers of the Midwest to the bold, spiky forms of Southwestern cacti. His use of indigenous plants was one of his legacies from the Arts and Crafts movement, which has experienced a renaissance in recent years, as people turned away from the stark Modernist dwellings and public buildings to personalized environments that preserve the best of the past. At this writing, interest in the multifaceted work of Frank Lloyd Wright has never been higher, as seen in an ever-growing list of books and articles, documentaries, reproductions and renovations of his endlessly creative designs. The plates that follow give some idea of the vista, breadth, and depth of his vision.

Below: The first Herbert Jacobs House, built in Madison, Wisconsin, in 1936, is historic in being Wright's first Usonian design. Brick wall masses carry most of the roof supports, and remaining walls are prefabricated of wood, faced with plywood on the interiors.

INTEGRITY OF SITE
AND STRUCTURE

Above: *The Midway Barns complex, with the dairy and machine sheds at center, was built on Wright's property in Spring Green, Wisconsin (1938–47), to help supply the needs of the Taliesin Fellowship.*

Page 16: *Fallingwater, Wright's residential masterpiece, is anchored in the native stone of the western Pennsylvania highlands.*

Wright's objectives remained consistent throughout his long career, although they were expressed in many different forms and materials. In *Two Lectures on Architecture*, published by the Art Institute of Chicago in 1930, he enlarged upon his definition of organic architecture, stating that "[The] sense of interior space made exterior as architecture transcended all that had gone before....The building now becomes a creation of interior space in light." These principles pervade his most memorable designs, both public and private.

Two early commercial buildings were especially noteworthy for their innovative use of the site/structure paradigm. The first was the Larkin Company Administration Building (1903) in Buffalo, New York—a commission that resulted from his acquaintance with his Oak Park neighbor and client William E. Martin,

whose brother, Darwin D. Martin, was a partner in the Larkin Company. This was a successful mail-order business located within Buffalo's grimy factory district, so Wright's office design effectively turned its back on its surroundings and focused on a central atrium skylighted from the top floor—an open workplace flanked by private offices in tiered galleries on either side. All of the order fulfillment was carried out in the atrium, which was also lighted by bands of windows at either end, creating a clean, quiet environment that was enhanced by several "firsts" in commercial architecture, including an air-conditioning system. This consisted of rooftop shafts that circulated fresh air through pipes located in utility wells at each corner of the building. To conserve interior space, all stairways and utilities were housed in these projecting features of the severe façade, which was ornamented only by symmetrical piers crowned by geometric sculptures created by Richard Bock. The building (demolished in 1949) was constructed primarily of fireproof brick, and Wright designed all of its furniture and fixtures.

Some fourteen years later, the architect devised an equally impressive and functional warehouse for businessman Albert D. German of Richland Center, Wisconsin, Wright's birthplace. The client had interests in commodities including coal, hay, grain, and cement (which he provided for the building). It utilized concrete-slab and brick construction and has flared column capitals similar to those on Oak Park's Unity Temple. The brick walls, nearly windowless, are crowned by an imposing concrete frieze in high relief, reminiscent of the work of Louis Sullivan, but executed in squares and rectangles rather than elaborate foliate patterns. This is Wright's only extant public building from the 1910s to employ sculptural ornamentation.

His native state, where he spent most of his life, is studded with other outstanding examples of Wright's work, notably the home/studio at Spring Green that he called Taliesin ("shining brow") in honor of his Welsh ancestry. His mother's family, the Lloyd Joneses, had been prosperous farmers here for generations, and Wright began to build in this serene Wisconsin River valley in 1911, after he had left his first wife, Catherine Tobin, for Mamah Borthwick Cheney, the wife of an Oak Park client. The ensuing scandal made it impossible for him to return to his practice in suburban Chicago, and Taliesin became both a home and a creative community that would grow to include the Hillside Studio and Theater (1902, 1932) and a working farm that helped to support the Taliesin Fellowship, where many prominent architects studied as apprentices from the early 1930s onward.

The house conformed to the crest of the hill on which it was built, primarily of

Below: This Prairie-style house on a hillside in Madison, Wisconsin, shows the strength of Wright's influence on residential architecture in his native state as practiced by Prairie School builders, many of whom had worked and studied with him.

native materials including limestone and timber, with low, cedar-shingled roofs. Both exterior and garden walls were laid up in irregular courses to resemble the stone outcroppings from which they had been quarried. The fluid plan of the complex was characteristically informal: many rooms opened onto flagstone terraces and balconies that overlooked the wooded countryside. Originally, the studio was at the center, with living quarters for draftsmen on one side and the main house on the other. Tragically, the original house was destroyed by an arsonist, who also claimed the lives of Wright's companion, both of her children, and four workers, in 1914.

Dazed by the shock and grief, Wright began to rebuild almost immediately, running deeply into debt in the process. A second fire, caused by an electrical storm in 1925, necessitated extensive renovation, but Taliesin continued to grow, forming a living laboratory of Wright's experiments in architecture. The house and grounds reflected his interest in Oriental art and design: the complex has secluded outdoor compounds and a spacious terrace with a roofed portico on stone piers, which frames the view from the hilltop. The Hillside Home School, which Wright had designed for his aunts Nell and Jane Lloyd Jones in 1903, was entirely remodeled in 1932 to provide a large drafting studio with housing for apprentices of the Taliesin Fellowship. Here Wright's concepts on urban planning for the future took shape in the large scale model called Broadacre City.

One of Wright's best-known commercial buildings is the S.C. Johnson & Son Administration Building (1936) located in Racine, Wisconsin. It was commissioned by Herbert F. (or "Hib") Johnson of the family-owned Johnson Wax Company, who admired Wright's work and became a close friend. His budget was $200,000—a huge sum for the Depression era—but the Wright charisma prevailed, and the landmark building came in at close to $3 million. Johnson was swept up by Wright's enthusiasm, expressed in his plan to make the complex "as inspiring a place to work in as any cathedral was in which to worship."

The half-acre Great Workroom, with its unique mushroom-shaped concrete columns, the streamlined glass tubing that replaced plate-glass windows, its walkways, and skylights, created an uncluttered and well-lighted interior for which Wright designed handsome contoured office furniture that is still in use today. The steel-and-wood desks and chairs harmonized with the restful terra-cotta color of the filing cabinets and other fixtures made to Wright's specifications. Some years later, he was called upon to build a multistory Research Tower for the expanding company, which was executed in the same alternating bands of brick and glass tubing. As the acclaimed architect Manfredo Tafuri said of the complex in *Modern Architecture* (Harry N. Abrams, 1979), "Its various elements emerge fluidly and without breaks from the enveloping forms of the buildings."

While the breakthrough commercial building at Racine was still under construction, Herbert Johnson asked Wright to design him a large country house at nearby Wind Point, a bold peninsula that juts into Lake Michigan. Wright envisioned the site as the ideal setting for the impressive house named Wingspread, which he was to describe as "the last of the prairie houses." The four wings spread out in pinwheel fashion from an imposing octagonal space that surrounds the 30-foot (9.1-meter) brick chimney core and soars toward three tiers of clerestory windows in the dome of the "wigwam," as Wright called the central living area. The outer walls comprise tall brick piers separated by 15-foot-high (4.6-meter) windows that lend an air of transparency to the building. This 40- by 60-foot (12.2- by 18.3-meter) area has four distinct zones on two levels, each with its own fireplace: a dining area, inglenook, library, and formal living room. The master-bedroom (north) wing extends over the east side of the living room to form a mezzanine, from which a spiral staircase ascends to the glazed observation tower on the roof.

The east wing was designed for four children—Mr. Johnson's son and daughter by his first marriage and the two sons of his young second wife, Jane Roach, who died before the house was completed. As Wright recalled in his autobiography, "Hib's interest in our building went way down. It took good persuasion to get him interested in ever going on with the house again…. I, friend now as well as architect, did my best to represent to him what I thought his young wife would wish were she living…. We completed the house in every particular as planned for a wife and four children. Hib seemed to sigh with relief upon seeing realized the home they had both worked on with me."

Below: The mushroom-shaped columns of the innovative, top-lighted Great Workroom at the S.C. Johnson & Son Administration Building in Racine, Wisconsin.

In an interview published by the *AIA Journal* for January 1979, Samuel C. Johnson described the pleasures of growing up at Wingspread, which now serves as an international conference center for the philanthropic Johnson Foundation: "I have many happy memories of living in this house: the pool and the young friends who came to see me; the pond where we could always catch a bass; the playroom which was adequate for any young man; the tower where we used to go up and play war games because you could see everything around—the whole site." Architectural historian Henry-Russell Hitchcock described the wings of the house (Wright's largest residential building) as "riding the grassed slopes as if they were floating on waves."

The intensely creative decade of the 1930s also saw construction of what is widely considered Wright's masterpiece:

Below: The bold, cantilevered profile of the elegant George D. Sturges House in Brentwood Heights, California, which was designed in 1939.

the Edgar J. Kaufmann, Sr., House known as Fallingwater (1936). One of the world's best-known private houses, it realizes Wright's lifelong ideal of a living place entirely at one with its setting—a wooded glen in the western Pennsylvania highlands threaded by a stream and waterfall. The Kaufmann family, owners of a thriving Pittsburgh department store, had used the site, called Mill Run, as a rustic weekend retreat for years before Edgar J. Kaufmann, Jr., an apprentice at Taliesin, brought his father and Wright together to design a country house here. The result far exceeded their expectations: a series of soaring cantilevered balconies anchored in solid rock and woven together by rough sandstone walls laid up in alternating courses. The southern exposure, with its glazed walls, faces the view of the stream, and the great stone-flagged living room has an open stairway that descends to water level just above the falls.

The house was built on three levels, with cantilevered terraces of reinforced concrete extending far out in four directions. Their mellow, buff-colored planes contrast effectively with the vertical shaft of mitered glass, sandstone, and steel that crowns the composition. Canopy slabs protect terraces and balconies from the elements and enhance the filtered light that illuminates the glen. The house's three bedrooms, kitchen, and utility areas comprise only a small proportion of the floor space, and in 1939 a guest house, with garage and servants' quarters, was added on a slope above the main house. It is accessed by a winding covered walkway made up of curved and geometric concrete forms. Similar forms encircle some of the trees in the garden—visual ribbons that link the complex and its setting.

In his later years, Wright designed several notable houses for his grown children, including the David Wright House (1950) in Phoenix, Arizona. This was primarily a circular Usonian house, the drawings for which were entitled "How to Live in the Southwest." The site was large and flat, surrounded by citrus orchards that obscured a distant view of Camelback Mountain. Wright's first concern was to raise the house on concrete piers to take in this view, with the added advantage of creating a shade garden below it through which cooling breezes could circulate.

Concrete block was the main construction material—an appropriate choice, since David Wright was in the concrete business. He was not an architect, like his brothers John and Lloyd, but his engineering skills were strong, and he served as general contractor for the house. He introduced the idea of including steel reinforcements and braces for the wooden roof, which have served well. The fact that his father was still hard at work on the spiral-shaped Guggenheim Museum in New York City probably influenced the design of this house, with its large spiral ramp to the entrance deck and a second ramp leading to the roof deck. A massive rounded chimney core begins at ground level and emerges through the roofline on one side of the cantilevered, single-story structure. The architect designed all the furnishings, including a handsome living-room rug with geometric circular motifs. They reprise the shape of this eminently livable house, which Wright called affectionately "David's treehouse."

Three years later, Wright was called upon to design a suburban dwelling for his youngest son, Robert Llewellyn Wright, who was an attorney practicing in Washington, D.C. The site was a wooded slope in Bethesda, Maryland, and the design was a variation on the theme of the solar hemicycle, Wright's first Usonian house, built for Herbert and Katherine Jacobs during the mid-1940s. Harking back to an even earlier period, Wright placed a continuous band of casement windows (which he favored for their ability to "bring the outside in") on both levels of the two-story, semicircular façade.

The primary building materials are concrete block and Philippine mahogany, which Wright used to dramatic effect as banding between the two floors and along the wide, flat roofline. The soffits (undersides of the eaves) extend widely over the second story and are surfaced in white to reflect light into the upper rooms. Contemporary as it is, the house recalls elements of the original Oak Park home and studio, which were in the Shingle style of the late nineteenth century. Wright had worked in this informal style during his apprenticeship to the architect Joseph Lyman Silsbee in 1887. Its affinity with the Arts and Crafts movement, a lifelong influence, may have affected his work on the 1953 house for his youngest son. The principal living areas, furnished entirely by Wright, open onto a private garden through glass doors. The masonry chimney core rises in graduated courses from a semicircular hearth very similar to that in the David Wright house.

The Johnsons of Racine were not the only clients who commissioned both commercial and residential designs in the Wright style. The architect also designed an elegant wood-paneled office, which is now installed in London's Victoria and Albert Museum, for Edgar J. Kaufmann, Sr., in his Pittsburgh department store, and

Above: The Arizona Biltmore Hotel (1927) was designed to meld with the sculpted desert landscape from which it rises as an oasis.

which conforms closely to its desert setting. A north-facing façade of concrete block laid up in protruding courses gives the horizontal house a strong vertical thrust at the center, where an open atrium is the focal point of both the common and private living areas.

The stark drama of the Southwestern landscape inspired some of Wright's most innovative work, including the Arizona Biltmore Hotel (1927), a little north of Phoenix, on which he collaborated with architect Albert McArthur, who had once worked as a draftsman at the Oak Park studio. Arizona hoped to vie with California and Florida as a mecca for wealthy Northerners in flight from the long, cold winters of their region, and the Biltmore project was key to attracting such a clientele. McArthur wanted Wright's advice on the textile-block construction he had used in California several years earlier for clients including Alice Madison Millard of Pasadena (La Miniatura, 1923) and John Storer (Los Angeles, 1924).

Clearly, Wright's influence on the Arizona Biltmore was substantial: the four-story main building uses alternating plain and patterned concrete blocks to create a regal presence, while the outlying wings, connected by textured covered walkways, link building and site into a coherent whole. The tile-ceilinged lobby is a spacious study in pierced and patterned columns massed to create indoor planters at various levels. It is illuminated by light cubes set into the concrete piers and a vibrant multicolored mural of saguaro cactus and other desert flora, originally designed as a cover for *Liberty* magazine. The effect is similar to that created in carved lava stone for the multilevel lobby of Tokyo's Imperial Hotel (1915–22).

an impressive house in Bartlesville, Oklahoma, for Harold C. Price, Jr., whose father had worked with Wright on the Price Company Tower headquarters for his pipeline business (1952). Oklahoma's flat terrain inspired a long, low structure with cantilevered balconies that raised it above ground level on a very gentle slope. The Prices called it "Hillside," and it does, indeed, form an airy, pleasing profile against the low planes and vast sky of its surroundings. It was completed in 1953, while Wright was designing a winter home for the senior Prices in Phoenix. His own experience in building Taliesin West in Scottsdale, Arizona, from 1937 onward, is reflected in this very large building (no longer in the family's possession),

Although many of his clients were wealthy industrialists and financiers, Wright never swerved from his desire to create attractive, livable housing for the average American—housing that he felt was consistent with the ideals of a democratic society. His humanist Unitarian background, and the Transcendentalist philosophy espoused by Ralph Waldo Emerson and Henry David Thoreau, imbued his thinking from an early age. So did the work of the English social theorist John Ruskin, which bore fruit in the Arts and Crafts movement. Thus many of his buildings, especially in the latter half of his career, were designed for clients of moderate means and employed prefabricated materials that were "personalized" to suit a given family's lifestyle. Among his extensive writings is *The Natural House*, published in 1954, when he had been designing such houses for several decades in diverse locations across the country.

The legend "A New Freedom," emblazoned against the backdrop for his model of Broadacre City, set the standard for these Usonian houses, each of which was tailored to its site. They were planned around five basic configurations, including rectangular, L- or T-shaped, hexagonal, single-block, and raised on masonry piers for steeply sloping grades. Examples include the Pope-Leighey House in Falls Church, Virginia, built on a rectangular plan with L-shaped wings (1939); the second house designed for Herbert and Katherine Jacobs, in Middleton, Wisconsin (1946)—set into a hilltop several feet below grade, with south-facing window walls along a semicircular façade—and the attractive Goetsch-Winckler House in Okemos, Michigan (1939). The latter was built at moderate cost for faculty members of Michigan State University, on a flat, wooded site that emphasizes the horizontal planes of the structure, with its triple-tiered cantilevered eaves. Brick, wood, and glass combine to form a simple, harmonious exterior that includes facing window-walls and a slender band of clerestory windows along the entryway. Many of these attractive, forward-looking homes are explored in the plates that follow.

Left: Striking geometric forms and a luxurious ambience made the Arizona Biltmore a showcase for newly emerging resorts in the Phoenix area.

AFLOAT IN THE DESERT *Previous pages*

A stark monolith on a rubblestone base signals the approach to Taliesin West, Wright's winter home/studio in Scottsdale, Arizona (1937–59). Its long, straight axis anchors the visionary complex to its isolated site, which now serves as headquarters for the Frank Lloyd Wright Foundation. Native materials and plantings accent the triangular elements inspired by the surrounding mountains.

SHAPED FOR THE FUTURE *Below*

Wright's last residential design was an essay in geometry based on the circle, which is a universal symbol of eternity. Reprising many of the elements he developed during his long career, this design was for the Norman Lykes House in Phoenix, Arizona. The house was not completed until 1967, eight years after the architect's death. Its curvilinear form closely follows the steeply rising site.

AN OPEN-AIR ROOFLINE *Above*

Wright designed houses for two generations of the Price family, this one as a retirement home for Harold Price, Sr., in Paradise Valley, Arizona. The atrium roof on this extensive concrete-block house is supported by inverted pylons inset with thin steel pipes to form a two-foot clerestory for air circulation and natural lighting. The fountain-cooled atrium divides the wings containing common and private spaces, respectively.

AN ARK-LIKE HOUSE OF WORSHIP *Opposite*
The steep triangular "prow" of the Unitarian Church in Shorewood Hills, Wisconsin (1947, interior, pages 38-39), juts boldly from a grassy slope, suggesting Noah's ark of salvation. The aging architect worked closely with fellow Unitarians to create this inspiring worship space for the Shorewood Hills congregation.

A VIEW FROM THE BRIDGE *Above*
The living room at Taliesin opens to the dramatic, cantilevered Birdwalk, which soars above the treetops to provide a breathtaking view of its Wisconsin River valley setting, including free-flowing streams and ornamental ponds created by damming. Both house and grounds reflect the architect's interest in Japanese design.

PACIFIC SHORELINE *Previous pages*

The house built for Mrs. Clinton Walker in Carmel, California (1948), has a broad roof supported mainly by the central chimney mass and continuous windows that open downward to admit sea breezes while excluding blown spray. Wright called the house (with typical modesty) a "tiny aristocrat among the Carmel bourgeois."

A MODERN-DAY MONUMENT *Right*

The Charles Ennis House (now the Ennis-Brown House) is the largest of the California textile-block residences of this period, built in Los Angeles in 1923. Plain and patterned concrete blocks alternate on the imposing exterior, while the multilevel interior has richly textured colonnades linking the various rooms and terraces. Mr. and Mrs. August Brown undertook much-needed restoration in 1968 and created the Trust for Preservation of Cultural Heritage to maintain the historic site.

A HOUSE FOR ALL SEASONS *Opposite and below*

Even when its waterfalls are stilled by winter, as in the detail opposite, Fallingwater retains its unique beauty above the picturesque stream called Mill Run in western Pennsylvania's unspoiled highlands.

FOCAL POINTS OF LIGHT   *Right*

The triangular sanctuary of the Unitarian Church in Shorewood Hills, Wisconsin (exterior, page 30), is flooded with sunlight; starlike points of light in the sloping ceiling carry out the theme.

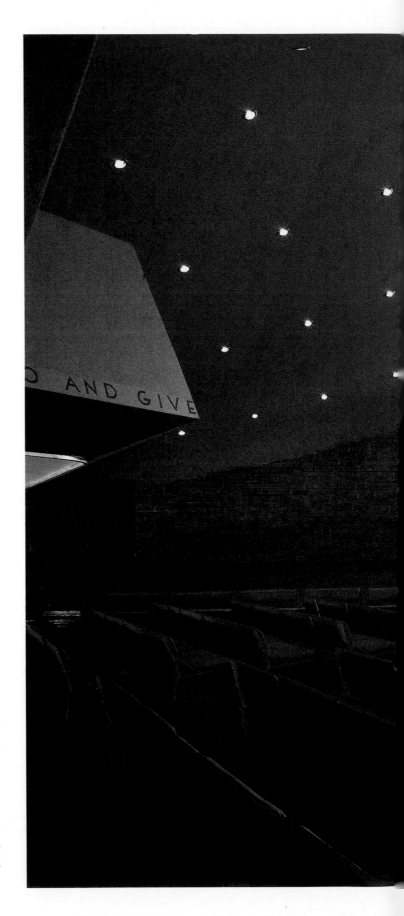

CIRCULAR SEGMENTS   *Page 40*

A closer view of the Norman Lykes House (page 28) shows the drum-shaped living room at right; the arc-shaped balcony that opens to the bedrooms; and the towerlike form of the master bedroom on the left.

AN INVITING APPROACH   *Page 41*

This graceful walkway ascends gradually to the beautiful main house at Taliesin, which Wright described as "not on the hill, but of the hill."

A PLACE IN THE SUN   *Pages 42–3*

A massive hearth of desert rubblestone anchors this colorful, comfortable gathering room at Taliesin West, in Scottsdale, Arizona: note the graceful "origami" chairs cushioned in blue (exterior, pages 26-7).

ARCHES ASCENDANT *Above and opposite*

Contorted evergreen branches frame a detail of the lights encircling the domed roof of California's Marin County Civic Center Administration Building (above). At right, spiky fans of palm contrast with the rounded forms of the Grady Gammage Memorial Auditorium at Tempe's Arizona State University.

COMMON AND
PRIVATE SPACES

Above: A portion of the lobby at the luxurious Arizona Biltmore Hotel, including the backlighted glass mural inspired by abstract forms of the indigenous saguaro cactus and other desert plants.

Page 46: A restful bedroom study at Taliesin, where the living quarters were rebuilt after a fire caused by an electrical storm in 1925.

Most of Frank Lloyd Wright's executed designs were for private houses and were concentrated in the Midwest—forty-three in his native Wisconsin and eighty-eight in Illinois, where he began his career in architecture and practiced until 1909. His houses, in all their varied forms, incorporated his ideal of the home as the stronghold of family life, often centered around a chimney core. This not only provided a gathering space for family and friends around the fireplace, but could serve as a visual screen that divided one common space from another, as in the recessed double hearth of the living/dining area in Chicago's Robie House.

In Wright's early houses, including his home in Oak Park, the fireplace was recessed in an inglenook and flanked by cushioned benches in the Arts and Crafts

manner, which drew heavily upon the Middle Ages for inspiration. In "showplace" common spaces that were designed for large-scale entertaining, like those for the Aline Barnsdall House and the Susan Lawrence Dana mansion in Springfield, Illinois, Wright experimented with massive sculptural hearths like the concrete fireplace in the Barnsdall living room, which combined the elements of fire and water in a reflecting pool at the base. He worked in such diverse materials as narrow Roman brick, rugged fieldstone, marble, lava stone, desert rubblestone, and the innovative textile blocks of the California houses of the 1920s.

Early in his career, Wright was often called upon to remodel an existing nineteenth-century house for clients whose needs or tastes had changed. Examples survive in Oak Park and other suburbs of Chicago, which expanded or sprang up in the wake of the great fire of 1871, which was followed by an unprecedented building boom. Many established Eastern architects came to the Midwest, including Joseph Lyman Silsbee, a skilled practitioner of Shingle-style architecture, which was influenced, in turn, by the work of the British architect Richard Norman Shaw, whose garden suburb at Bedford Park, London (1876), was the first of its kind and became a model.

One of Wright's first independent remodeling commissions was for the Harrison P. Young House on Oak Park's North Kenilworth Avenue (1895). The additions he designed for the front of the house required moving it back 16 feet (4.9 meters) to accommodate a living room, a long verandah, and two second-story bedrooms. Built on the original foundations, the north end of the verandah, covered in narrow clapboards, cantilevers over the driveway; the living room, which extends across the entire front elevation, has windows onto the verandah for maximum light. In this early example are several features that would become Wright style signatures: the concept of "zoning," whereby large common spaces are grouped separately from the kitchen, pantry, and other utility areas as well as from the bedrooms; the use of screening—in this case, Tuscan columns and spindles—rather than solid walls to permit a freer flow of space; and distinctive fireplaces. The Young House has two: one in the living room, the other in the master bedroom. Their oak mantels rise in widening tiers, with beaded woodwork that is reprised in the den as egg-and-dart detailing. The fireplace surrounds are of narrow glazed Roman brick with rounded corners.

The imposing Nathan G. Moore House (1895) in Oak Park represents Wright's unique approach to the style requested by his client—Tudor Revival, which the architect deplored as derivative and outdated. However, he needed the work, and Moore was both a friend and neighbor. The house designed for him had the tall, stacked chimneys and horizontal half-timbering of its medieval predecessors, but Wright added an all-American porch with a low balustrade on the south (garden) side.

Below: Dining in splendor at the Arizona Biltmore, which was designed to make Phoenix a wealthy resort area on a par with Palm Beach, Florida, and Palm Springs, California.

49

Above: *The southern exposure of the Nathan G. Moore House in Oak Park, as remodeled in 1923, is even more imposing than the original cross-gabled, Tudor-style design of 1895.*

Somehow, it merged seamlessly with the steeply pitched rooflines and peaked gables. It was an unusually large house, with a reception room, library, and conservatory on the ground floor, as well as a spacious living room, dining room, kitchen, and butler's pantry. Two of the six upstairs bedrooms shared a balcony, and traceried Gothic windows formed attractive bays. Moore was well satisfied with the house, which met his stipulation that "We don't want you giving us anything like that house you did for Winslow" (in nearby River Forest). Wright got his second chance at the Moore House, however, after it was ravaged by fire in 1922. The horizontal trim disappeared, and the roof was extended downward to the line of the first-floor lintel, its original tiles replaced by slate.

Massive horizontal chimney-stacks at right angles displaced the towering Tudor-style chimneys, and pierced screening in the Japanese mode framed the projecting windows of the façade, giving this impressive house, with its adjacent stable, a new ambience, complete with terra-cotta panels and Sullivanesque ornamentation. Charles E. White, who had worked with Wright before opening his own practice, supervised construction of the renovated dwelling.

Nathan G. Moore was literally the moving force behind another historic Oak Park house, this one at 313 North Forest Avenue. The Hills-DeCaro House was originally a Victorian-style residence, which Moore relocated to its present site in 1906. Wright was commissioned to remodel it for Moore's daughter Mary and her husband, Edward R. Hills. He remade the structure in the Prairie style that he had evolved by the turn of the twentieth century, including ribbons of casement windows, stucco surfacing with wooden stringcourses (bands) that emphasize the horizontal, and a multilevel roofline with extremely broad eaves. The house was heavily damaged by fire in 1976 and meticulously restored by its new owners, the DeCaros, with the help of architect John D. Tilton. Burnished wooden floors, Wright-designed furniture, and an art-glass bay window on the landing between the first and second floors contribute to the strength and serenity of this house, as re-created by Wright and rescued some seventy years later.

Early in the twentieth century, Wright had the opportunity to design two houses for Francis W. Little: a T-shaped Prairie-style residence with a stable, located in Peoria, Illinois (built 1902), and the innovative "Northome" on Minnesota's Lake Minnetonka (1912, demolished 1972). Its 55-foot (16.8-meter) living room was probably the largest interior of the Prairie period and certainly one of the most impressive. The house commanded a beautiful view of the lake's Robinson Bay and of the natural woodlands behind the site. The main-floor dining room had bedrooms above it, while other sleeping quarters were on both floors—an unusual plan for Wright, who usually configured private spaces on an upper story or in a separate wing. Privacy was a priority in his residential designs, from the compressed, sometimes concealed, main entrances to master bedrooms, bed- and playrooms for children, dens, offices, and libraries. Even in large houses, these "retiring rooms" were often quite small and simply fur-

nished, providing a sense of enclosure. In his later houses, mitered windows that wrapped around a corner of the room contributed a sense of transparency, connecting the occupant with an attractive landscape feature like a grove of trees or a sweep of meadow. Burnished wood paneling, soothing colors, and low lighting all contribute to the ambience of these private spaces, which Wright considered essential to a harmonious dynamic among family members, couples, and companions.

The uncluttered site of the Little House in Deephaven, Minnesota, eventually became crowded with other buildings that spoiled the view, but when it was demolished, several important rooms were preserved. Thanks to architect and Wright historian Thomas A. Heinz, the living room was eventually reconstructed in the American Wing of New York's Metropolitan Museum of Art. (An authority on Wright's work, Mr. Heinz has made

Below: Vertical trim on the steep end gable of the Moore House emphasizes the vertical thrust of the building as it overhangs the stone-tracery bay window at ground level.

Above: Shallow pedestaled urns like this one set on a low pier at the Darwin D. Martin House in Buffalo, New York (1904), were a Wright design signature in the first phase of his career.

more than 50,000 photographs of his architecture, which appear in his own books and those of other writers on this subject.) Northome's library was rescued by the Allentown, Pennsylvania, Art Museum, where it now opens onto an enclosed courtyard.

Among Wright's most successful Prairie House designs are those he developed for large sites like that of the Darwin D. Martin House in Buffalo, New York (1904). Many of these included ancillary buildings that were integrated into the site plan and visually unified with the central structure while preserving their functional autonomy. Unfortunately, the race to develop more housing on less space, which began after World War II, has adversely affected many of the larger sites that now house only remnants of Wright's original

plans. At the Martin House, for example, the spacious conservatory and its glassed-in, 100-foot (30-meter) connecting gallery, as well as the gardens, stable, and garage were demolished. The Wright historian William Allin Storrer reported in 1978 that "apartment buildings now crowd the lot."

On a more positive note, the George Barton residence, adjacent to the Martin property, was kept intact and restored by Eric Larrabee and his wife, Eleanor Larrabee, an architect. The Martin House itself has recently undergone extensive renovation under the auspices of its present owner, the State University of New York at Buffalo, and the nearby Alexander Davidson House (1908) has been lovingly restored by Gregory Kinsman. In an estimated year-long project that turned into a four-year job because of hidden structural problems, the enterprising renovator removed thirty-two leaded-glass windows, some of which had to be replicated by a local art-glass specialist, and tackled the problems created by years of neglect. The longleaf-pine floors and cypress trim were refinished to their original mellow beauty before the windows were reinstalled. Unable to afford original Wright furnishings, Mr. Kinsman built his own "in the Arts and Crafts style, like the architect sometimes used in his smaller houses."

A similar labor of love was undertaken by architect Albert H. Clark and his wife, Georgianna Clark, in 1975, when they purchased the single-story Usonian house built for J.A. Sweeton in Cherry Hill, New Jersey. Its red floor of concrete slab was designed to provide radiant heat, and the interior was surfaced with red plywood board-and-batten. The original roof comprised two-foot (0.6-meter) lengths of overlapping boards, subsequently replaced by shingling. Laid out on a square module, the house has a truncated T-style plan, with an extension for additional workspace off the master bedroom. When the Clarks began their renovation twenty-five years later, they had a hard time matching the original construction materials, including plywood, brick, and concrete block with flush vertical grouting and recessed horizontal grouting. As in many of Wright's houses, the cantilevered fireplace tended to smoke when the fire died down. The Clarks finally decided to seal it, observing wryly that "Now it's more a piece of sculpture." The carport (which was a Wright invention) is also cantilevered—a contemporary version of the porte-cochere that once allowed family and guests to get into and out of their carriages near an entrance in unfavorable weather.

In 1909 two architects who had trained with Wright, Barry Byrne and Andrew Willatzen, brought the emergent Prairie School of architecture to the Northwest when they established their practice in Seattle. One of their first major commissions was to design a summer home for lumberman Albert S. Kerry, who was determined to put Seattle on the map with the help of the Alaska Yukon Pacific Exposition of 1909. "Glenkerrie" represented a new approach to Northwestern housing—the refined, progressive presence of the typical Prairie House, with its low-pitched, cross-gabled roofs; broad overhangs that helped shed heavy rainfall; and geometric designs carried through from the stained-glass lighting fixtures to window mullions and gateposts.

The original plan, with a terrace-framed living room extending from the front (east) elevation, could not be built in its entirety because of financial constraints, but Willatzen was called back in 1928 to finish the house much as it had been designed in 1910. Subsequent alterations compromised his detailing, and changes in contemporary lifestyles brought a new look to the kitchen area and former servants' quarters when Kerry's great-grandson modified the Prairie-style house to his family's needs. As reported by Lawrence Kreisman of The Seattle Times (February 20, 2000): "The kitchen was at odds with the rest of the house, where symmetry and axial relationships were so important. It was a cavernous space, designed when families of means had live-in help, and big enough to accommodate the kind of entertaining [Albert S.] Kerry had expected to do after enlarging the house. Architect Todd Heistuman of Seattle was challenged to remodel the kitchen as if Willatzen had

designed it for a household without servants. The new kitchen is symmetrical, its central axis lined up to the center of the band of windows." The former servants' quarters were turned into new private spaces: a den and a study. Renovations of this kind were entirely in keeping with Wright's principles of organic architecture, which grows and changes to meet the needs of the times. His associates, from the original Oak Park Studio to the enduring Taliesin Fellowship, have been instrumental in promulgating these principles to the present day.

Many impressive projects were developed during the late 1920s, only to remain unbuilt at the onset of the Depression. One of them was an innovative complex called San Marcos-in-the-Desert, designed, like the Arizona Biltmore, to make the state attractive as a winter resort on the order of Palm Springs, California, and Florida's elegant Gold Coast. However, the time Wright spent in Arizona was not wasted. He discovered a deep affinity for the desert landscape and the possibilities it opened up for new types of living space. After establishing the informal Ocatillo Camp in Chandler as a base for work on San Marcos-in-the-Desert, he designed the prototype Chandler Block House—a small unit to be constructed partly from prefabricated elements at moderate cost. It reflected his lifelong interest in affordable housing that turned its back on congested, overbuilt cities, which would germinate into the 1931 model of Broadacre City and an influential book entitled *The Disappearing City*, which stated his case against the International Style.

He was especially critical of the towering glass skyscrapers on concrete stilts that jammed the streets of Manhattan, Chicago, and other major metropolises,

creating an environment that he considered ugly and dehumanizing. The desert opened up new vistas, and Ocatillo Camp became the predecessor of Taliesin West, the winter home/studio built by Wright and members of the Taliesin Fellowship beginning in 1937. As explored more fully in chapter 5, this complex would continue to grow and evolve under the leadership of architects including Bruce Brooks Pfeiffer of the Frank Lloyd Wright Foundation. Meanwhile, despite his diatribes against the International Style, it is interesting to note that many of its leading lights acknowledged their debt to Wright, whose work was included in an exhibition of the style at New York City's Museum of Modern Art in 1943.

Writing, lecturing, and teaching filled much of Wright's time during the early 1930s, when money for new construction was scarce. He published the first edition of his memoirs, *An Autobiography*, in 1932 with Longmans, Green & Company, thus making a new generation aware of his work at a time when many thought that his career was over. (True to his tendency to reinvent himself as well as his work, a second edition of his autobiography—revised and enlarged—appeared in 1943, published by Duell, Sloan & Pearce.) His mind and his beloved draftsman's pencils remained active throughout an apparently fallow period, and by the mid-1930s his career was reascendant. One of its first fruits was the landmark Hanna House, designed for Paul R. and Jean Hanna in 1936 in Palo Alto, California.

Wright's young clients had followed his work for some years, and when Paul Hanna joined the faculty of Stanford University in 1935, the couple asked for a house within their means, to be built on

Opposite: Dramatic triangular trusses in the Hillside Drafting Studio at Taliesin evoke the tools of the architect's trade.

a hillside overlooking the campus. They worked closely with the architect on the innovative design, which was based on a hexagonal model that gave rise to the nickname "Honeycomb House." Built primarily of brick, copper, and glass, the house had alternately high and low ceilings. Precast hexagonal tiles were laid down as flooring on a concrete base, and the walls followed the intersection of the floor lines. Extensive outdoor terraces increased the living space and were both visible and accessible through glass doors, sections of which were designed to fold away to the sides and effectively disappear. California redwood was used to create a warm interior, in which every detail was designed by Wright to accommodate the hexagonal plan.

Some twenty years later, when the three Hanna children had grown up, Wright was called back to remodel the house to fit the family's changing needs. He added a guest house and a workshop and altered the interior to provide fewer, but larger, rooms. The terraced garden is memorable, graced by broad stone steps, the play of water jets, and a two-ton urn of carved lava stone, which Professor Hanna imported from Tokyo before the demolition of the Imperial Hotel in 1968. Six years later, the Hannas deeded the house to Stanford University, and soon afterward the Nissan Motor Company contributed three million dollars to its endowment, as a gesture of appreciation for Wright's lifelong interest in Japanese culture.

The original Hanna House was nearly complete when Wright designed a landmark residence for Ben Rebhuhn in Great Neck, Long Island, New York (1937). Thomas A. Heinz has called it "the missing link between the Prairie and the later Usonian designs. The low-pitched roofs with broad overhangs are evident, as are the clean red brick and cypress cladding." Especially striking is a bold cantilevered plane that projects over the garden, pierced by three large rectangles that admit light in the manner of a trelliswork pergola. The house is based on a cruciform plan and has a two-story living room with glazed walls overlooking the handsome wooded site.

Another notable residence from this productive decade is the George D. Sturges House in Brentwood Heights, California (1939). The building is cantilevered over a narrow brick base, which gives it the appearance of floating above its sloping site. It faces south to give a panoramic view of the Pacific Ocean, with the entry at the back. The house was built with two bedrooms adjacent to the living room on the east side, which opens to a balcony overlooking the street below.

The house designed for Loren Pope in 1940 (now the Pope-Leighy House) was a milestone in several respects. Originally located in Falls Church, Virginia, it recalls the first built Usonian—the Herbert Jacobs residence, in Madison, Wisconsin (1936). It became widely known when Mr. Pope, a journalist in Washington, D.C., wrote an article for *House Beautiful* describing the economical use of space in his new home, which was of horizontal cypress batten construction around a brick core. Many readers were inspired to write to the architect requesting similar houses of their own, and after the World War II moratorium on building ended in 1945, Wright's practice was rejuvenated yet again. The house was moved to its present site in Mount Vernon, Virginia, in 1964 and is now owned by the National Trust for Historic Preservation.

Opposite: Jewel-like tones of green, gold, and amber pervade this serene view of the winter garden at dusk from the Meyer May House in Grand Rapids, Michigan.

CLEAN LINES *Previous pages*

The classical proportions of the Robie House living room show Wright's genius for reinterpreting the past in ways that were relevant to twentieth-century needs. As he wrote of his work in 1931, "At no point does it involve denial of the elemental law and order inherent in all great architecture; rather, it is a declaration of love for the spirit of that law and order" (*In the Cause of Architecture*).

OPEN SPACES *Opposite and above*

Two views of the eminently livable common space at Fallingwater identify it as a country house, from the polished-flagstone floors to the colorful modular furnishings of the various seating areas, grouped to take full advantage of the views on all sides. Natural boulders on the site (below, right) were incorporated into the design of the hearth.

THE SOLAR HEMICYCLE *Left*

The Kenneth Laurent House in Rockford, Illinois, is a graceful semicircular Usonian facing into the garden pool and terrace. Red brick and Tidewater cypress are the principal construction materials, and the innovative built-in furnishings allow a clear path through the single-story house, designed in 1949 for a client who was confined to a wheelchair.

THE USONIAN AUTOMATIC *Right*

What Wright called his Usonian Automatic building system involved the use of large concrete blocks made from
local materials, many of which were found on the site, to
keep costs low. The living room of the Gerald Tonkens
House in Amberley Village, Ohio, probably the largest
example of this type of residence (1955), shows that econ-
omy was no impediment to style and comfort.

AT HOME WITH ARTWORK *Overleaf*

The concrete-block Eric V. Brown House, one of the four
built for employees of the Upjohn Corporation at Parkwyn
Village, in Kalamazoo, Michigan, provided ample shelving
for the owner's art collection, set off to good advantage by
unpatterned blocks, a warm mahogany ceiling, and flexible
units of modular plywood furniture (1949).

A USONIAN LANDMARK *Opposite and above*

The L-shaped house built for newspaperman Loren Pope in Falls Church, Virginia (1939), was widely publicized by the client's article in *House Beautiful*, which praised such innovative features as the jigsawed fretwork screening and clerestory (detail above) and the economical use of space on a small site. The Wright-designed plywood furniture was adaptable to a large single grouping or configured as smaller units throughout the living room. Now known as the Pope-Leighy House, the residence was acquired by the National Trust in 1963 and removed to Mount Vernon, Virginia.

A PLACE FOR EVERYTHING *Overleaf*

The harmonious Melvyn Maxwell Smith House (exterior, page 168) is based on a plan devised by Wright from photographs and a topographic survey of the Bloomfield Hills, Michigan, site sent by Mr. Smith in 1946 after his discharge from service in World War II. He and his wife Sara mastered the details of Usonian construction and did much of the work themselves. This is the last Usonian house that utilizes full board-and-batten construction, as illustrated by the ceiling treatment and the exterior view. From this point onward, most Usonians were of masonry construction, with wood paneling on the interiors.

SHADES OF RED AND GOLD *Right*
This view of the William Palmer House living room in Ann Arbor, Michigan, highlights the warm effect achieved by combining cypress with sand-mold brick and glossy flooring incised with the house's triangular grid.

ETCHED IN GEOMETRIC FORMS *Previous pages*
Pages 72-3: The impressive reception room in the long outbuilding at Auldbrass Plantation is part of the complex designed for agricultural research by the client, Leigh Stevens, on his large property in Yamassee, South Carolina.

Page 74: A rectangular clerestory and wooden paneling distinguish this hallway that opens to the living room of the Tonkens House in Amberley Village, Ohio (1954).

Page 75: Frank Lloyd Wright's secluded study at Taliesin in Spring Green commands a comprehensive view of the Wisconsin countryside.

A TAPESTRY IN GLASS *Overleaf*

Wright surpassed himself in his renowned art-glass designs for the Meyer May House, in Grand Rapids, Michigan, as seen here in the shimmering bay of the living room, with its copper-sheathed window detailing.

A MUSICAL VENUE *Opposite & below*

This handsome Usonian living space was designed for Dr. Isadore Zimmerman of Manchester, New Hampshire, in 1952 with a focus on the musical events that the Zimmermans held regularly for their circle of friends.

A MASTERFUL COLLABORATION *Opposite & below*
Architect Marion Mahoney, the first female graduate of the School of Architecture at the Massachusetts Institute of Technology, worked closely with Wright on the impeccable design of the Meyer May House and all its furnishings and fittings. On the opposite page is a detail of the living room; below, the art-glass doors to the verandah.

LOOKING UP *Previous pages*
Page 82: Detail, art-glass windows and skylight in the Frank W. Thomas House, Oak Park (1901). Page 83: The intricate, glittering fanlight at the entrance to the Dana-Thomas House in Springfield, Illinois (1902), was executed to Wright's design by Chicago's Linden Glass Company.

USONIAN LIGHT SCREENS *Overleaf*
Fretwork cypress screens and ceiling lights give continuity and pattern to the living/dining area of the Melvyn Maxwell Smith House in Bloomfield Hills, Michigan.

SERENE, SCULPTURAL VISTAS *Opposite & above*

Red-glazed brick, Georgia cypress, and clear glass comprise the 36-foot-long (11.0-meter) living room of the Isadore Zimmerman House (opposite) and the elegant dining area above. The concrete floors are sealed with Colorundum, a water-repellant material available in many colors.

COMPRESSED ENTRYWAYS *Opposite*

Wright created a sense of expectation about his living spaces by approaching them obliquely, as seen in this narrow hallway and diagonal wall that opens up to the spacious living room of the Palmer House in Ann Arbor, Michigan.

NEW DIRECTIONS IN FURNISHING *Above*

The barrel-shaped, cushioned chairs that flank the rectangular table in Taliesin's dining area are among Wright's best-known designs—and provide much more comfortable seating than some of his earlier tall-backed spindle chairs.

IN THE ROUND *Right, detail above*

This spacious conservatory in the William H. Winslow House (1893) is adjacent to the dining room. Oak columns define the continuous band of windows, which have clear-glass center panes surrounded by delicate patterns that recall the work of William Morris. It seems appropriate that Winslow and Wright collaborated on the publication of William C. Gannett's "The House Beautiful" here in 1896. Winslow's limited-edition Auvergne Press was housed in the large Wright-designed stable on the property.

THE ESSENTIAL FIREPLACE *Opposite & below*

Wright's emphasis on the fireplace as "the heart of the house" is illustrated below by the Arts and Crafts-style inglenook with built-in benches in his own Oak Park living room and by the much larger double-tier brick fan surrounding the hearth at the nearby Arthur Heurtley House (1902), shown on the opposite page.

DISTINCTIVE OVERHEAD LIGHTING *Overleaf*

Among Wright's design signatures is the use of elegant recessed lighting in the ceilings of his common spaces, including the F.F. Tomek House dining room in Riverside, Illinois (page 96), designed in 1907, and the unique art-glass panels in the dark wooden trusses of the Heurtley House living room (page 97), which follow the form of the hipped roof.

GEOMETRIC CHIMNEY CORES *Opposite & below*

The rounded brick chimney core of the multilevel common space at Wingspread (opposite) soars past the triple clerestory to the rooftop observatory of this remarkable country house, now the headquarters of the H.F. Johnson Foundation. Below is the rectangular Roman-brick fireplace of the G.C. Stockman House in Mason City, Iowa, which looks so contemporary that it is difficult to believe it was designed in 1908.

MULTILEVEL
INTERIORS

Above & page 100:

The two-story octagonal library is part of the studio added to the Frank Lloyd Wright Home in 1898, at left in the exterior photograph shown above. The young architect met with clients in this innovative, top-lighted room with its handsome spindlework furniture and Arts and Crafts-style ornamentation.

Wright's five-year term of employment with Adler & Sullivan saw him increasingly involved in the partners' commissions for residential architecture, since they focused on large commercial contracts like those for Chicago's landmark Auditorium Building and the famous Wainwright Building in St. Louis (1890). Dankmar Adler's strength was in the realm of business and finance, while Louis Sullivan became perhaps the foremost exponent of the Chicago School, producing 120 buildings. His skyscrapers were innovative and influential in their steel-skeleton construction, vertical articulation, and intricate low-relief ornamentation based on models from nature. Wright was deeply influenced by Sullivan, both personally and professionally, and worked with him on the sumptuous Golden Door for the Transportation Building at the World's Columbian Exposition held in Chicago in 1893 and other large projects.

Wright's talent was immediately apparent, and the firm quickly assigned most of its residential commissions to him, although he was not always credited with a principal role in these designs. For Chicago's James Charnley House (1891), for example, Sullivan's initial concept was amplified and refined by Wright in a residence that the British writer Robert McCarter has described as "one of the greatest works of architecture of its period, surpassing the similar urban houses of Wright's mature contemporaries McKim, Mead and White...an absolutely astonishing work for an architect not yet twenty-four" (*Frank Lloyd Wright,* Phaidon Press, 1997).

Built of brick, the Charnley House rises from a wide base of smooth ashlar stone that lifts at the center to frame the entryway, which is crowned by an ornamental loggia. The window openings were left unframed, and the façade is plain, apart from the cornice and loggia; the interior is consistent in its simplicity, comprising a three-part plan centered on the skylit central hall that carries the stairway to the top of the house. Now the headquarters of the Society of Architectural Historians, the house bears the unmistakable imprint of Sullivan's vertical thrust and distinctive ornament combined with Wright's innovative concepts of interior space, which would result in a new American architecture.

Another early essay in multilevel dwelling spaces was a row of four identical urban townhouses, built for Robert W. Roloson (1894) on Chicago's south side. Tan brick with ashlar trim, the houses rise to steep medieval-style gables, each with a stone-framed frieze between the second and third floors. The interiors were designed on the mezzanine principle that would appear so often in later works—the central stairwell is the dividing point, and floor heights vary from the rooms along the façade to those at the back of the houses, ensuring privacy. Wright spoke to the theme of the urban rowhouse years later in a 1935 issue of *Taliesin*, a periodic publication of the Taliesin Fellowship, addressing several features that had been anticipated in the Roloson Apartments decades before. Proposing a "zoned house" suited to city life, he observed that "The townhouse is tall; all rooms have high ceilings. The entire house is hermetically sealed from dirt and noise…. The slumber zone is introduced as mezzanine, with [a] balcony opening into the living kitchen." In keeping with the zone principle, he recommended that a utility stack house all the wiring, plumbing, and heating components and that outdoor living space be provided in the form of a rooftop garden "where greenery can see the sky."

Lower-cost urban accommodation was designed by Wright as early as 1895 in the form of Francisco Terrace, built for Edward C. Waller on the corner of Chicago's Francisco and West Walnut Streets. In this two-story brick complex with stone trim, all of the apartments except those on the street side opened onto a rectangular courtyard reached through a Richardsonian-style archway of terra cotta. Conceived as affordable housing for working-class renters, the courtyard was accessible to all the inside apartments via a balcony that connected with stairwells in open towers at each corner of the building. (Similar utility towers would soon appear in the plans for Oak Park's Unity Temple and for Buffalo's atrium-style Larkin Building.) As with any pilot project, unanticipated difficulties developed, notably the noise level of traffic on the wooden balcony, which was amplified by the courtyard. However, the building was occupied for decades before it fell into disrepair and was eventually demolished (in 1974). Fortunately, the entrance arch, framed by foliate designs in the Sullivanesque style, was dismantled and reconstructed on Euclid Place, in Oak Park, several years later. There it remains as part of the Frank Lloyd Wright Prairie School National Historic District, including twenty-five of his buildings and a rich variety of renovated Prairie-style and Victorian-era houses.

After his break with Sullivan, Wright maintained an office at Steinway Hall, Chicago, with other like-minded young architects, some trained by Sullivan, others by Wright himself after he opened his own Oak Park studio in 1899. There, gifted associates including Walter Burley Griffin, Marion Mahoney, and Walter Drummond became involved in the decade of intense creativity that began at the turn of the twentieth century. Happy clients referred others, and national publication of Wright's designs, plus accolades from European architects, resulted in a thriving practice that reached beyond the Chicago area to encompass Wisconsin, Michigan, Indiana, Ohio, Iowa, and New York State.

Several major commissions of 1901 saw the Prairie House emerge into full realization, as seen in the Ward W. Willits House in Highland Park, Illinois, which conforms to Wright's stated objectives: "The prairie has a beauty of its own and we should recognize and accentuate this natural beauty, its quiet level. Hence, gently sloping roofs, low proportions, quiet sky lines, suppressed heavy-set chimneys and sheltering overhangs, low terraces

Below: The imposing Dana-Thomas House dining room as seen from the balcony, including the semicircular bay with built-in seating used for less formal gatherings.

and out-reaching walls sequestering private gardens." The Willits House is constructed mainly of wood and steel, with exterior plastering and wood trim. All the living quarters are raised above ground level, and the wings of the house radiate from the central core—a massive fireplace with wood screening— like a pinwheel. The main floor includes the entry hall, dining room, living room (with a glazed end wall overlooking the terrace and grounds), and the kitchen, adjoined by the servants' rooms. The upper floor houses all the family bedrooms. Wright historian William Allin Storrer illustrates the floor plan, in which the porte-cochere, extending from the entry-hall wing, is balanced by the long porch off the dining room. He observes of the Willits House that "From this concept, the Prairie ideal would develop to more open, yet interlocked spaces," as seen in the Robie House of 1906, described in the following chapter.

The mansion designed in 1902 for the heiress Susan Lawrence Dana (now the Dana-Thomas House) in Springfield, Illinois, was Wright's largest residential commission to that date. His client was an art collector who entertained on a lavish scale, and she requested a large new house that would incorporate her Italianate family residence while providing much-needed space for her collection and the prominent residents of the Illinois capital whom she entertained in her capacity as a patroness of the arts. The imposing house that Wright created was under construction for several years and eventually comprised thirty-five rooms, three of which were two stories high: the gallery (1905), dining room, and reception hall. The gallery was connected to the house by a covered passage that also served as a conservatory.

Built on a cruciform plan, like the Willits House, this Springfield landmark has all of its principal common spaces on the first floor and bedrooms on the second. The original first-floor library, with its marble fireplace bearing a butterfly design, was converted into a parlor, while the butterfly motif was carried through in the chandeliers Wright designed for the dining room and gallery. Gifted collaborators including sculptor Richard Bock, artist George Niedecken, and the Linden Glass Company were closely involved with the project, which resulted in some 450 pieces of exquisite art glass bearing abstract designs of the prairie sumac in warm, autumnal colors. The art-glass windows in the master bedroom form part of a larger composition created by the living-room windows on the ground floor. The beautiful dining room, with its barrel-vaulted ceiling, was designed to seat up to forty guests and has a recessed bay with built-in seating for smaller groups. In 1944 publisher Charles C. Thomas purchased the house and assumed responsibility for preserving it as Wright had designed it, including all the furniture and fittings. Designated a National Historic Landmark in 1976, the Dana-Thomas house was purchased by the State of Illinois (1981), which retained architect Wilbert Hasbrouck of Hasbrouck Peterson Associates to undertake major restoration work on the property.

Like so many of Wright's buildings, the Dana-Thomas House has a sculptural quality that is hard to capture in even the finest photographs: it invites one to view it from all sides to appreciate fully every aspect of its coherence from the inside out. As Robert McCarter has pointed out: "In our age of computer animation and information, virtual reality, and the dis-

embodying influence of film and television, all sense of place—and even the need for places to house human life—is increasingly at risk of disappearing....In our age of biography, where emphasis is placed on the process and practically no notice taken of the product, any understanding of the architect's intentions as they are constructed in the actual built work seems increasingly irrelevant. By substituting information apprehended by viewing and reading for the direct physical experience, these two aspects of our contemporary world view impede our access to Wright's spaces, which were designed to be understood through occupation."

Above: Wright's creative use of varying ceiling and window levels to define separate interior spaces within a coherent whole is illustrated in this view of the entrance hall of the Gerald B. Tonkens House, Amberley Village, Ohio, built in 1954.

Below: An imposing galleried space in the S.C. Johnson & Son Administration Building, in which the sleek, modern design is softened by the use of curvilinear forms, natural light and an unusual midlevel display of plantings.

Several lakeside dwellings from this first phase of Wright's career deserve mention for their effective combination of multi-level spaces on wooded sites designed to provide a refuge from the increasing noise and pollution of inner cities. The Charles Ross House on Lake Delavan, Wisconsin (1902), is notable for the fact that rooms which Wright had previously opened up to one another by removing the walls between them were reconfigured so that the living spaces overlap and interpenetrate one another—a new variation on the cruciform plan that extends toward the four points of the compass.

The A.P. Johnson House (1905), also in Lake Delavan, is a prototypical Prairie House with a multilevel hipped roofline and bold piers extending into the grounds. The massive central fieldstone chimney unmistakably defines the main portion of this handsome two-story house, with its upper-level casement windows and a Roman-brick fireplace. Reportedly, Wright and his client were alienated because of changes made without the architect's knowledge during the last stages of construction, and it was not until 1971 that a new owner, Robert Wright (not related to the architect), took steps to conform the house more closely to its original design.

The boldly conceived Thomas Hardy House (1905), in Racine, Wisconsin, was also designed for a lakeside site, on a steep embankment overlooking Lake Michigan. The central section is a large, three-story square, with smaller squares inset on each side. The street-side elevation is defined by a continuous band of rectangular art-glass windows on the ground floor, restated above as larger, square windows below the roofline, with each stucco "panel" articulated by vertical banding. Entrances are at either end of the house.

The two-story living room faces the lake and is flanked by bedrooms that open to walled gardens. Wright's associate Marion Mahoney made a brilliant perspective of the Hardy House as seen from Lake Michigan, with a central terrace flanked by anchoring piers that jut from the hillside. Unusually for this period of Wright's work, the dining room is on the ground floor, overlooking the terrace, with the living room above it. The simple grandeur of the house as it rises in tiers from the embankment is fully expressed in this lakeside elevation.

The 1910s brought new variations on spatial themes that Wright had experimented with since he began his career as a draftsman in 1886. Many designs from this decade went into the archives as unbuilt projects, often because they were considered too revolutionary, or overly expensive, by his prospective clients. However, Wright never wasted a good idea, and many built projects were "shaken out of his sleeve," as he put it, and adapted to new sites and circumstances.

After his return from Europe in 1911, Wright's compositions took on a new authority that was often expressed in looser, less formal, designs. His country home/studio in Spring Green, Wisconsin, is an exemplar of this development. As he said of this unique complex in his mother's ancestral "Jones Valley," "Every time I come back here it is with the feeling that there is nothing anywhere better than this." Now a National Historic Landmark, Taliesin includes the Hillside Home School, with its drafting studio, theater, and gallery of design; the shingle-clad Romeo and Juliet windmill (1896), composed of both octagonal and diamond-shaped forms that merge to reinforce one another; the Midway Farm complex; and the Wright-designed Visitor Center, which encompasses the only extant restaurant designed by the architect (created in 1953 for the Wisconsin River Development Corporation). Crowning this Wisconsin River valley is the fluid house and studio that follows the crest of the hill, framing the view of the natural beauty that had imprinted itself upon Wright's consciousness in childhood. As mentioned earlier, Taliesin was a work in progress from 1911 until 1959, the year of his death.

The dwelling is built of native materials including limestone and timber, with low, cedar-shingled roofs and plaster surfacing. The common rooms flow into one another and open to terraces, gardens, and pavilions that reveal Wright's affinity for Japanese architecture and design. Originally, the house and studio were some 7,000 square feet (650 square meters) in extent, but today Taliesin is more than five times that size, although many features were carried over from one stage of construction to the next. The stone wall of the living/dining area has a high-ceilinged bedroom behind it with rich furnishings and textiles whose motifs appear in various forms throughout the house. The surround of the limestone fireplace, laid up to resemble the natural out-

Above: The single spiral ramp ascending gradually from ground level at New York City's groundbreaking Solomon R. Guggenheim Museum deconstructed conventional modes of dividing vertical space.

croppings from which it was quarried, flows seamlessly into the rugged stone wall on either side. A six-paneled Japanese screen above the bed reprises a similar screen in the living room, and the ceiling is trimmed in the same way. Oriental themes and materials figure prominently in decorative objects of art throughout the house and grounds. During his maiden voyage to Japan, with his first wife Catherine and the Ward Willitses in 1905, Wright took many photographs of the island nation's temples, shrines, waterfalls, gardens, and cities and added to his growing collection of Japanese prints.

Wright's well-known interest in Japan was instrumental in securing the commission for the lavish Imperial Hotel in Tokyo (1916–22)—one of his most influential buildings of the period following World War I. It was designed to replace an outdated German hotel of the same name, and

the fee was $300,000—a staggering sum for the time, and one that Wright needed to meet his mounting debts at Taliesin. His personal life had remained in crisis since the tragic deaths of Mamah Borthwick Cheney and her children, and the crisis was compounded by an ill-advised liaison with the poet Miriam Noel, whom he later married and divorced. He sailed for Tokyo at the end of 1916 and spent much of the next seven years in Japan, leaving his son, architect Lloyd Wright, to finalize American commissions already in hand.

The frequent earthquakes to which the Japanese islands are subject made it imperative to do massive site preparation in the form of concrete pins driven deeply into the mud underlying the surface soil, which was 60 to 70 feet (18 to 21 meters) deep. The outer walls were of brick, reinforced with concrete and steel, and designed to rise from a massive base line

Below: The inviting reception hall in the William H. Winslow House (1893), in River Forest, Illinois. Note the delicate arcade across the private raised area on the left and the Sullivanesque frieze of stone and plaster.

to a thinner upper level, to keep the center of gravity low. The hotel was laid out on an axial plan, with simply furnished guest rooms in wings flanking the multilevel lobby, which had a grand entrance reflected in an ornamental pool. The imposing lobby was built of brick and carved lava stone (oya) and carpeted with textiles handwoven in China to Wright's specifications. In all, the architect produced more than 700 drawings for the project, including furniture, sculpture, murals, tableware, glass, and upholstery fabrics. The intricately detailed structure occupied a full city block and proved its soundness by surviving the devastating earthquake that struck Tokyo and Yokohama in 1923. It stood until 1968, when it was demolished to make room for yet another grand hotel. Fortunately, portions of it, including the lobby, were reconstructed in Nagoya's Meiji Mura Museum, an architectural park featuring buildings from the Meiji era.

Among Wright's other public buildings are notable houses of worship for various faith communities. They reflect his liberal Unitarian beliefs, which respect the principles underlying all religions and the dignity of humankind as manifested in the diversity of our cultures, beliefs, and value systems. In fact, the legend inscribed on his historic Unity Temple is implicit in all of his ecclesiastical buildings: "For the Worship of God and the Service of Man." He worked closely with the ministers and congregations for whom he undertook these commissions, studying the history of their liturgies, symbols, and objects of veneration through the centuries to make the buildings he designed expressive of their spiritual roots. Space permits us to describe only a few of the most outstanding works of his later period.

Above: A cleverly designed balcony overlooks the simple lines of the living room in the Herman T. Mossberg House (1948), located in South Bend, Indiana.

Above: Wright's affinity for geometric forms is clearly seen in this view of Unity Temple, designed for the Unitarian congregation of Oak Park in 1904.

The hexagonal Annie Merner Pfeiffer Chapel (1939) at the Florida Southern College in Lakeland was an integral part of Wright's plan for the campus of this small Methodist college devoted to the liberal arts. Its president, Ludd Spivey, had engaged Wright's interest with his request for help in designing a "college of tomorrow," built on a lake surrounded by citrus orchards. The chapel's skylighted bell tower strikes a vertical note on the campus, where most of the other buildings are low, connected by covered esplanades and inset with colored glass that reflects the tropical sunlight in a manner reminiscent of stained glass. Like its companion build-

ings, the chapel is built mainly of reinforced cast concrete and sand-cast concrete blocks containing local limestone formed of indigenous shells and corals. Multilevel ceiling heights help define the hexagonal form of the structure, in which the pulpit projects from a triangular stage toward the seating area. The bell tower soars beyond the pierced-concrete screen of the choir loft to fill the worship space with light. Minimal ornamentation beyond that incorporated into the structural materials pervades the chapel with a powerful sense of unity and repose.

In designing the beautiful Beth Sholom Synagogue of 1954 in Elkins Park, Pennsylvania, Wright worked hand in hand with Rabbi Mortimer J. Cohen, who envisioned the temple as "a mountain of light" symbolic of Mount Sinai, where the Ten Commandments were revealed to Moses. The synagogue rises from a hexagonal base to form a massive tentlike structure suspended from a 160-ton tripod of steel and concrete, which creates an unobstructed sanctuary that can seat more than 1,000 worshippers. Walls of aluminum, glass, and fiberglass filter natural light into the sanctuary during daylight hours, and the whole structure glows with interior lighting by night.

The great triangular canopy over the main entrance symbolizes hands joined in blessing over the congregation, and the interior slopes gently toward its focal point—the sacred ark that contains the Torah. The motif of the light-giving menorah recurs on both the exterior and the interior of the building, while a remarkable chandelier of colored glass, like a winged triangle, is suspended above the congregation, symbolizing the inexpressible attributes of the Divine. Rabbi

Cohen's contribution to this house of worship for his people was so great that he is credited on the plans as codesigner. He was deeply grieved by Wright's death, which occurred only five months before the dedication of the temple. This transcendent house of worship is one of the seventeen structures designated by the American Institute of Architects to be retained as examples of Wright's contribution to American culture.

Wright's last ecclesiastical commission was the Annunciation Greek Orthodox Church (1956), Wauwatosa, Wisconsin. Here Wright enlisted the help of his third wife, Olgivanna Lazovitch, a native of Montenegro who had been raised in the Greek Orthodox faith, as well as his own knowledge of Byzantine architecture, which he admired deeply. In this contemporary worship space, he combined the primary symbols of the faith community: the dome and the Greek cross, which has arms of equal length. The ground plan is formed by the Greek cross inscribed in a circle, which rises to the upper part of the building on piers of cast concrete. Here a bowl-shaped balcony ringed by glazed arches provides natural overhead light, and is crowned by the shallow dome of the roof.

The circular theme is carried out in the building's interior gilded metalwork, including the delicate iconostasis, or icon screen, before the altar. A second seating level is formed by the curving lines of the balcony below the domed ceiling. The precast, perforated sunscreen that encircles the roofline like a crown is sharply pointed, recalling the paramount Byzantine theme of Christ Triumphant, as seen in icons and mosaics at Istanbul's Hagia Sophia and other citadels of the Greek Orthodox faith. The primary color throughout is gold, another attribute of kingship. The British-born architect Donald W. Hoppen, who studied with Wright at Taliesin, has observed that with the convex forms of Annunciation, Wright achieved "a new dimension of spatial energy" (*The Seven Ages of Frank Lloyd Wright,* Capra Press, 1993).

Left: The circular form of the Annunciation Church is reprised in the graceful curves of the balcony and windows as well as in the abstract motifs of the iconostasis before the altar.

CLASSICAL INFLUENCES *Pages 112 & 113*

Two rooms from the late 1800s show how Wright merged classicism and modernism in his early work. On page 112 is a view into the Winslow House dining room through a graceful arch framed by the living-room frieze. Page 113 shows the barrel-vaulted playroom added to the architect's Oak Park Home in 1893. The balcony level, highlighted by the *Winged Victory of Samothrace* above the archway, enhances, but does not dominate, the two-story space.

A SCHOLAR'S RETREAT *Right*

Designed in 1939 for two faculty members of Michigan State University, the Goetsch-Winckler House in Okemos has a large, broadly defined living area that encompasses the kitchen workspace, the dining table adjacent to the chimney, and the book-lined living room, with its comfortable, flexible furnishings. Two bands of clerestory windows overlook the wooded site of this impressive Usonian house.

SERENITY IN REPOSE *Left*

The two-story music room at Taliesin is a richly textured composition of textiles, murals, pierced screening, modular furniture, recessed lighting, and native stone.

REACHING NEW HEIGHTS *Pages 116 & 117*

Two views of the great octagonal living space designed for the Herbert F. Johnson House, Wingspread, in Wind Point, Wisconsin. Page 116: One of the five gathering spaces grouped at different levels around the massive three-story chimney; each has its own fireplace. On page 117 is a detail of the spiral staircase that rises from the balcony past the triple clerestory to the rooftop observatory.

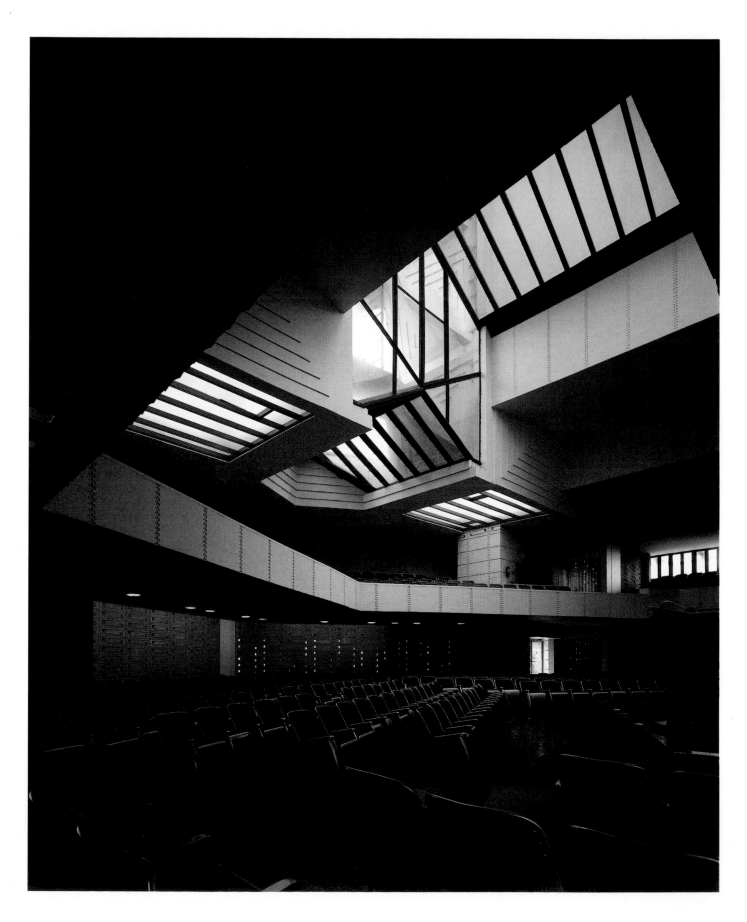

A SKYLIT WORSHIP SPACE *Opposite & above*

The Annie Merner Pfeiffer Chapel at Lakeland's Florida Southern College (1938) was designed for what its president called "the college of tomorrow." Its bell tower is a breezeway-shaped skylight that ascends on steel supports to the highest point on the campus. The choir takes its place on the balcony (above), which is screened by a lattice of slender, patterned concrete blocks.

STUDIES IN PERSPECTIVE *Overleaf*

Contrasting angles in two early twentieth-century Illinois homes. On page 122, the wood trim and neutral colors of the Prairie-style Ward W. Willits House (1901), Highland Park, are accented here with an art glass panel. Page 123 shows an aspect from the balcony overlooking this comfortable, well-lit seating area at the Isabel Roberts House (1908) in River Forest.

SANCTUARY, UNITY TEMPLE *Previous pages*

This multilevel worship space is focused on the pulpit and the organ screen, cleanly defined by horizontal and vertical banding, geometric hanging lamps, and the art-glass clerestory. The coffered skylights have an amber tint. The dignity and restraint of this church is in total accord with the spirit of the Unitarian faith community, of which the architect was a member.

A SENSE OF EXPECTATION *Below & opposite*

In the Dana-Thomas House, below, the indirect entrance to the elegant gallery sets the scene for artistry with its intricate chandelier, glazed walls, and sculptural ornament. On the opposite page, the interior of the Rollin Furbeck House (1897) in Oak Park flows toward the upper level on a wide, graceful stairwell integral with the balustrade along the balcony above.

CONTEMPORARY GRANDEUR *Left*

The formal dining room and adjacent breakfast area in the E.E. Boynton House (Rochester, New York, 1908) exemplifies the Prairie-style interior at its best. William Allin Storrer observes that this is "a particularly fine space, graciously large, with plentiful lighting including a large clerestory and overhead light panels. The dining table, seating eight to fourteen, is supportd by four posts surmounted by lights of simple yet elegant geometry."

INFUSED WITH DRAMA   *Right & overleaf*

The living room at Taliesin, in its third and final form, is a microcosm of Wright's experiments in architecture throughout his long career. The Japanese influence is unmistakable in the ornamental screens, artwork, and translucent panels, while built-in seating alternates with early high-backed and "barrel" chairs and the modular units of the later period. On page 132 is the colorful Taliesin Hillside Theater (1952), where the Fellowship and guests gathered for plays, films, and lectures. A balcony dining room overlooks the stage.

SOUTHERN STYLE, UPDATED   *Page 133*

The boldly appointed hexagonal kitchen at Auldbrass Plantation in Yemassee, South Carolina, is separated from the main house by a long gallery—a feature that dates back to Colonial days, in which this helped to accommodate the region's hot, humid climate.

NATIONAL HISTORIC LANDMARKS   *Pages 134 & 135*

Page 134 shows the north-facing view of the Dana-Thomas House Gallery, designed as a separate pavilion for the mansion commissioned by heiress Susan Lawrence Dana in 1902. On the facing page is a view of the ceiling and art glass windows of the unique Robie House living/dining area as seen from the central stairwell.

"CHILD OF THE SUN" *Previous pages*
Wright's name for Florida Southern College in Lakeland reflected his ideal of an educational institution designed for twentieth-century American students, in stark contrast to the ivy-covered Gothic towers dictated by tradition. Many students helped defray the cost of their tuition by participating in the construction of the ambitious multibuilding complex. Its primary materials are concrete block, steel, brick, and glass, and its interiors are functional, light and spacious.

A SPIRALING MONUMENT TO MODERN ART *Opposite & below*
New York City's controversial Solomon R. Guggenheim Museum, originally designed in 1943, encountered many obstacles before it finally opened in 1959. Its radical form—an expanding spiral ramp that visitors traverse to view the collector's comprehensive objects of modern art—was both praised and damned by critics, but the museum's unique form, from domed skylight to spacious central court, has proved ideal for its purpose and made it a world-famous Manhattan landmark.

SHELTERING EAVES AND BALCONIES

Above and page 140:
Steep Gothic gables pierced by elegant windows with a Japanese motif distinguish the Nathan G. Moore House (1895) in Oak Park (baluster detail above). The second floor was altered and restored by Wright after a fire in 1922.

Among the earliest manifestations of Wright's stated intention to "break out of the box" of traditional residential design in the late nineteenth century was the movement away from tall, narrow houses and restrictive cubes toward more flexible spaces that opened up from the inside to the outside. Early essays in what would become the Prairie House showed an increasing emphasis on the horizontal versus the vertical, as reflected in low, multilevel rooflines with broad eaves, and winglike balconies and terraces that increased the sense of spaciousness without compromising the privacy of the inhabitants. This design hallmark evolved from early residences for the suburbs of Chicago to both city and country houses, as well as commercial and ecclesiastical commissions.

As Wright's sphere of influence expanded, his work began to attract favorable attention from European architects, who compared him to the young Josef Olbrich of Vienna's Secessionist School. American architects and would-be homebuilders learned of his work by word of mouth, local examples of his style and widespread publication of his ideas (he was a prolific writer as well as a charismatic speaker). However, not everyone was captivated by his work. In a 1953 article for *The New York Times,* Wright tells an amusing story of himself as a young eavesdropper on critics of the William H. Winslow house when it was under construction in 1894: "I remember climbing up into an upper part of the building to listen to comments. In came a young fellow with a couple of young women and the fellow said, 'Have you seen the man who built this? God, he looks as if he had a pain.' Another one said, 'They say this cost $30,000, but I can't see it.' I learned my lesson: I never listened like that again."

Critics notwithstanding, Wright made it a lifelong practice to supervise the construction of his buildings whenever possible, and the results speak for themselves in painstaking attention to every detail. By 1901 his Prairie style had matured to a high point exemplified in the Ward W. Willits House in Highland Park, Illinois. The primary construction materials were wood and steel, with exterior plastering and horizontal wood trim. All the living quarters are raised above ground level on a foundation and base course of cement. The living room has a glazed end wall that overlooks a large terrace and the landscaping beyond it, and the wings of the house fan out in pinwheel fashion from the central core—a massive fireplace with wood screening that defines the various public spaces on the ground floor without cutting them off from one another. A long, low porte-cochere that extends from the entry-hall wing is balanced by a long porch off the dining room. Ribbons of leaded-glass clerestory windows bring light and color to the interior with the help of the projecting eaves, whose undersides are flat and white to help reflect natural daylight. All of the family bedrooms are on the second floor, with servants' quarters adjoining the kitchen on the ground floor. The Willits House conforms to Wright's goals for organic architecture, as outlined in his autobiography: "a new sense of repose in flat planes and quiet streamline effects." As such, it is one of the seventeen Wright buildings designated for preservation by the American Institute of Architects.

Wright's first Prairie-style house in Oak Park was also designed in 1901: the Frank W. Thomas House, commissioned by James C. Rogers as a gift to his daughter and son-in-law. Like most of Wright's houses, this one has no excavated basement. The plan is L-shaped, with all the family living areas on the raised first floor and the bedrooms on the second level. Rooflines on the lower story project over the porch and the dining room on either end of the house. Widely spaced casement windows on the second floor have broad overhangs from the shallow hipped roof, which is crowned by a long, low brick chimney. The entrance is notable for its cleanly defined archway, flanked by low walls that contribute a sense of privacy. For some years, the

Below: A balcony framed by renowned art-glass windows ornaments the landmark Avery Coonley House (built 1907) in Riverside, Illinois.

Above: The influence of the Austrian Secessionists is apparent in the ascending planes of the clearly articulated William E. Martin House (1902) in Oak Park.

original plaster façade was obscured by shingling, but this was removed in 1975 during a faithful restoration. Intricate art glass and recessed ceiling lights add to the beauty of the spacious interior.

The best-known of all the Prairie houses is the Frederick C. Robie House (1906), which was designed for a narrow city lot in Chicago for inventor Frederick Robie. The client contributed to the advanced technology incorporated into what has been called "the house of the century." He worked closely with the architect, alloting a generous budget that included Wright-designed furniture, fittings, utility systems and landscaping. When the house was built, it had a distant view of the prairieland around fast-growing Chicago; today it is owned by the University of Chicago and is part of its campus. Interestingly, the site is near that of the classically inspired World's Columbian Exposition of 1893, where

Wright worked on the Transportation Building with his mentor Louis Sullivan. As Thomas A. Heinz points out: "Wright saw buildings at this fair that affected him throughout his life but at the same time consolidated his modernist tendencies, which was in part due to his employer at the time….Designed by Adler & Sullivan, the Transportation Building was virtually the only major exposition building that was non-classical and non-white."

The Robie House is built along a horizontal axis, lengthened by the cantilevered roof, which extends above the west verandah some 20 feet (6.1 meters) beyond its masonry supports. Brick and concrete are the primary construction materials, and the long, low structure is free of ornamentation, except for the concrete banding that accents the horizontal line. Multiple porches and balconies provide access to the outdoors on several levels, giving the house a silhouette that has been compared to that of a steamship. Privacy was enhanced by locating the entries out of the sight line from the street.

The three-story house has its principal common rooms on the main (second) floor, where there are no walls or partitions to break the flow of space through the living/dining areas and the central stairwell. On this level, a brick fireplace with flues on either side and an opening above the mantel serve as a screen rather than a divider. The southern exposure, opening to a long balcony, is lined by art-glass French doors for natural daylight; overhead, glass globes in square brackets provide nighttime illumination. Both ends of the common space terminate in diamond-shaped bays. The kitchen and servants' quarters are in line along the back of the house.

On the ground floor, a playroom for the Robies' young children opened onto a walled courtyard, and a billiards room served as a recreation area for social gatherings. Here again, utilities like the boiler room and the laundry were grouped at the back, adjacent to a built-in garage—a major innovation for the period. The third floor housed the children's bedroom, a guest room, and the master bedroom suite. The enterprising young client contributed many ideas that helped to create the efficient lighting system, telephone and alarm systems, and an industrial-type vacuum-cleaning installation. The house cost some $60,000 when it was built and has been declared a National Historic Landmark.

Isabel Roberts was a valuable member of the Oak Park Studio staff, and Wright designed a house for her in nearby River Forest in 1908. Its cruciform plan can be seen from the street in the narrow living-room wing, which rises one-and-one-half stories to the balcony that overlooks it.

The other three wings housed a covered porch, the dining room, and the utilities, respectively, while the upstairs balcony opened to three bedrooms and a bath. For some time, the original stucco surface banded in wood was covered by a brick veneer, but in 1955, new owner Warren Scott engaged Wright to remodel the house. He restored the plaster surfacing, replaced the roofing material with copper, and used blond Philippine mahogany for the interior woodwork throughout. Much of the living space was reconfigured, but the diamond-paned casement windows were retained, and the tree that was enclosed by the original porch is still an unusual feature of this distinguished house.

Below: Strong octagonal towers with conical roofs flank the entry to Oak Park's George W. Furbeck House (1897). They reflect Wright's affinity for the octagonal form during his early period, as seen in the library addition to his nearby Studio.

A landmark design from 1908 is that of the Meyer May House in Grand Rapids, Michigan, where Wright was given a free hand to implement his ideas on unity and cohesiveness throughout the project. Here he experimented with ornamental latticework that screens the first-floor windows from the street and drew the eaves well out over the building's extensive terraces. Light-colored brick piers crowned with urns and planters extend the house into the substantial grounds.

Inside, the May House conforms to the criteria that Wright would set down a year later in the Wasmuth Portfolio, prepared for publication in Germany (*Ausgeführte Bauten und Entwurfe von Frank Lloyd Wright*): "It is quite impossible to consider the building one thing, and its furnishings another, its setting and environs still another. In the spirit in which these buildings are conceived, these are all one thing, to be foreseen and provided for in the nature of the structure." The living spaces unfold into one another in the form of burnished woodwork, softly diffused light from elegant art-glass windows and symmetrical fixtures, carpets in warm autumnal colors, glowing murals, and the essential living-room hearth, with its three tiers of brickwork. The dining-room table, encircled by Wright's favored high-backed chairs, has a short pier at each corner to uphold square art-glass lamps whose design echoes that of the windows, carpets, and textiles.

The logical extension of the organic house was the organic community, which appears conceptually in many unbuilt projects and was first carried out in part at the Ravine Bluffs real-estate development in Glencoe, Illinois. Attorney Sherman M. Booth, who acted on Wright's behalf for some years, purchased a large, hilly tract near Lake Michigan in 1911 with ambitious plans for a residence of his own, a number of Wright-designed houses for rental, and a handsome bridge (recently restored) over the deep ravine that gave the project its name. To mark the boundaries of the property, several distinctive poured-concrete sculptures incorporating massive rounded urns and art-glass finials were executed, probably by Wright's frequent collaborator Alfonso Ianelli.

The architect's original L-shaped plan for the Sherman M. Booth House was extremely large, with massive stucco surfaces, numerous balconies, and multilevel rooflines. For reasons unknown to us—perhaps financial exigencies—Booth chose not to build this house, but to remodel several smaller buildings on the site, one in 1911, the second in 1915. The result was a relatively modest multilevel Prairie house, with stucco surfacing and horizontal wood trim. A three-story bedroom section was added, and an existing garage and stable were connected. All five of the smaller houses in the project were based on Wright's adaptable 1907 plan for *The Ladies' Home Journal* entitled "A Fireproof House for $5,000." Each has a square plan divided in half through the center to form a large living room on one side of the ground floor and a dining room and kitchen on the other. The central stairwell projects from the plan to reach the private level upstairs, with three or four bedrooms and a bath. The houses are not identical, as in so many post–World War II developments of the Levittown type. They are distinguished by various roof pitches, placement of the street-side elevations, and location of their porches and entrances. Although designed as rentals, the houses were soon purchased by owners whose names are still used to identify them today: Charles Perry, Frank B. Finch, C.J. Ellis, J.M. Compton, and S.J. Gilfillan.

By this time, Wright was deeply involved in planning the Imperial Hotel for Tokyo—his largest commission to that date and one that required long absences in Japan. While there, he designed several residences for Japanese clients and the Jiyu Gakuen School in Tokyo (1921), which has a central pavilion flanked by wings of classrooms. His familiarity with Japanese culture is apparent in his 1912 book *The Japanese Print, An Interpretation*. Here, the illustrations show the use of continuous horizontal wooden bands at the door-top level to delineate the wall space above and below and other aspects of the Japanese folk house that became more pronounced in his later Usonian buildings, many of which reflect the observation by architect Tadao Ando that "A Japanese can make a whole life in a small space."

In 1928 Wright married his third wife, Olgivanna Lazovitch, who would have a

Below: The enclosed, pier-lighted stairwell to the raised living space of the Frank W. Thomas House in Oak Park (1901) is sheltered by a covered porch.

marked influence on the rest of his career, which many considered to be over at this point. Now in his mid-sixties, the architect completed only five buildings during the years 1925-32, and the list of unbuilt projects from this period is long and disheartening, due mainly to financial constraints, including the onset of the Great Depression. However, we have seen that he reached new heights from the mid-1930s onward, beginning with the Edgar J. Kaufmann, Sr., House, Fallingwater, in 1936.

One house that marked the transition between the Prairie and Usonian styles is the Malcolm E. Willey residence, designed and redesigned beginning in 1933. Located in Minneapolis, Minnesota, the Willey House, originally planned as a two-story residence, was reduced to a single story, with a cantilevered upper deck enclosed by a wooden parapet and a pergolalike projection of pierced cypress wood over the terrace. The principal construction materials are dark-red sand and paving bricks, while the warmly colored cypress would become a favored material for Usonian houses of the future. As Wright historian William Allin Storrer points out, the newly evolved "central workspace," combining the kitchen and utilities core, directly adjoins the living-dining room—another feature typical of the standard Usonian, except that it would be L-shaped, with the workspace at the juncture of the living room and the gallery.

A notable house in the new style was designed in 1946, after the World War II moratorium on construction, for Melvin Maxwell Smith in Bloomfield Hills, Michigan. According to Thomas A. Heinz, "The Smith house [on 3 acres of ground] has one of the loveliest and most serene settings of any of the Usonian houses, and a small lake visited by blue herons can be seen from nearly every room." An L-shaped house built mainly of brick and cypress, it faces into the garden at the rear and was enlarged by Taliesin Associated Architects in 1969–70. It closely follows the model of the second house built for the Herbert Jacobs family (called Jacobs II) in Middleton, Wisconsin (1943). A solar hemicycle, this attractive two-story house, with bedrooms on the second level, has an open ground-floor plan that includes a circular tower beside the kitchen housing the stairwell and the second-floor bath.

Two Usonian essays in community planning were undertaken in the late 1940s for the employees of the Upjohn Company: Parkwyn Village, in Kalamazoo, and the Country Home Acres development in Galesburg, both in southern Michigan. Wright's plan for both was based on a series of circular grids, which proved difficult to implement along conventional property lines. Only four Wright-designed houses, all of concrete-block construction, were eventually built in the proposed forty-lot Parkwyn Village, for Robert Winn, Ward McCartney, Eric V. Brown, and Robert Levin. Cleanly defined roof cantilevers provided patterns of light and shade on the pierced and patterned blocks, similar to those used for the Arizona Biltmore Hotel. In Galesburg, too, the futuristic planned community eventually included only four Wright houses, one of which was the two-story Curtis Meyer House (1950), designed as a series of semicircles with a flat roof whose broad eaves follow the countour of the house. Concrete block and mahogany (now weathered to a beautiful patina) were the principal construction materials.

The Henry J. Neils House (1950) in Minneapolis is an unusual Usonian in that Neils was in the building-products business and wanted the residence built of granite and scrap marble with aluminum windows—a rare example of metal windows in a Wright house, but successfully carried out in multiple clerestories that contrast with the subtly colored granite blocks. A series of gabled rooflines shingled with cedar extends from a large carport at one end to the central section, defined by a massive stone chimney, to the living-room wing with adjacent triangular terrace.

The Isaac N. Hagan House (1954) in Chalkhill, Pennsylvania, may serve as a final example of Wright's mature residential style. This imposing house is built mainly of sandstone, with a copper roof whose widespread overhang is pierced by geometric forms that are reminiscent of those used for the contemporaneous Annunciation Greek Orthodox Church. Eminently livable, the house appears to grow from its hillside site, commanding a wide view of the surrounding countryside. The living and dining areas are floored with flagstone, and the adjacent central workspace with cork tile. The entry is in this wing, while the bedrooms and bath extend past a graveled courtyard to the carport. All the furniture was designed by Wright, and the working drawings were prepared by John H. Howe. Fire damage sustained after completion was fully repaired by the second owner, Peter Palumbo.

Below: The multilevel Robie House (1906), with its raised terraces and broad eaves, was designed to provide free access to the outdoors without loss of privacy on an urban lot in Chicago.

TEXTURAL CONTRASTS *Opposite*

The smooth buff-colored eaves and balconies of Fallingwater work hand in hand with the roughly textured native sandstone, as seen in this view of the "floating" staircase that descends from the living room to a pool formed just above the waterfall. The striking sculpture on the low courtyard wall is the work of the French artist Jacques Lipchitz.

A MONUMENTAL PRESENCE *Above*

Unity Temple, in Oak Park, rises from a low, projecting base to a slab roof of waterproof concrete that juts out over the rectangular masses and decorative columns of the façade. On a practical note, the thick walls of this Unitarian church served to muffle the noise of the nearby streetcar line.

ABOVE IT ALL *Overleaf*

This dramatic textile-block balcony on the John Storer House seems to be suspended among the mature plantings of its steep Hollywood, California, site like a fantasy treehouse. The house commands an incomparable view of Los Angeles.

THE ESSENCE OF SHELTER *Above and right*

Rectangular walls of brick and matching block roofed with cypress (right) form a secure vantage point from which to view the winter garden at the William Palmer House in Ann Arbor, Michigan (1950). The soaring diagonals of the triangular roofline (above) form the ceiling of the living/dining area.

AN OPEN INVITATION *Overleaf*

The famous living room at Taliesin extends onto the cantilevered Birdwalk that overlooks the property's luxuriant natural setting along the Wisconsin River.

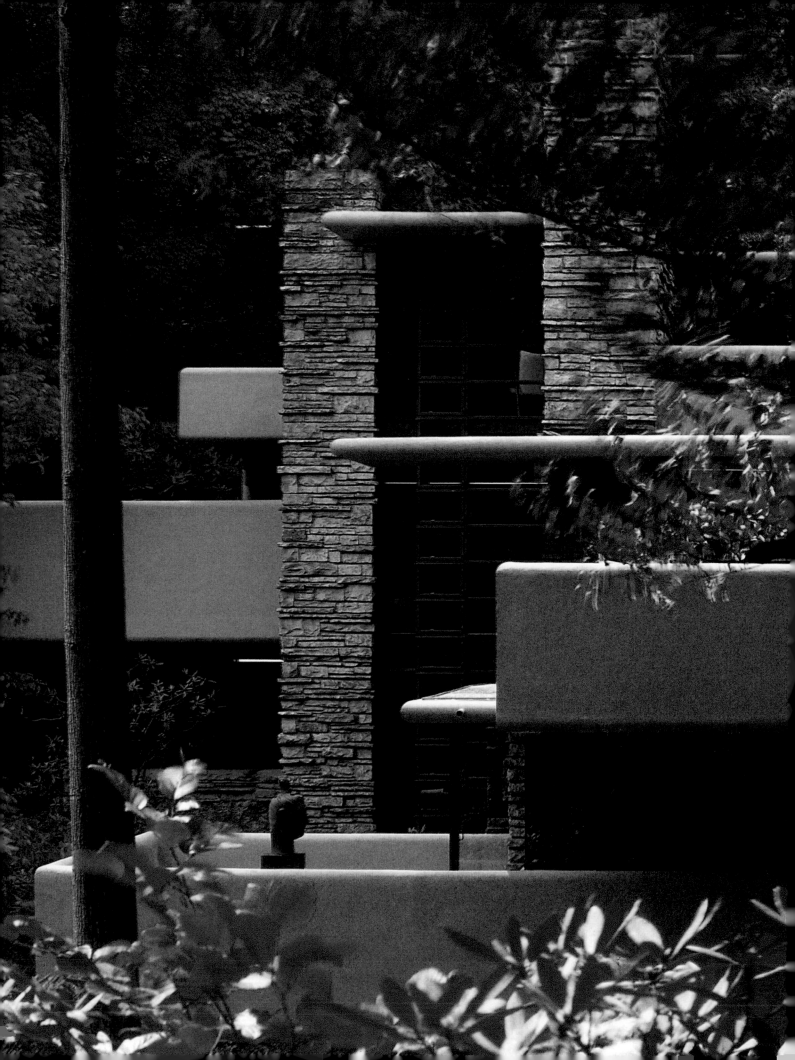

THE WRIGHT MATERIALS *Previous pages*

On pages 158-59, the full-height sandstone window-wall framed in Cherokee-red steel adds vertical thrust to the horizontal masonry planes of Fallingwater.

Pages 160-61: The low-pitched, upturned copper eaves of the Dana-Thomas House have aged to a green patina that highlights the façade of narrow Roman brick, stone, and the art-glass ribbon windows. Note the rich Sullivanesque frieze in the detail on page 161.

Pages 162-63: Roman brick reappears on the multi-level Robie House, alternating with limestone coping free of ornamentation. The cantilevered roofline contributes to the play of light and shadow in this detail.

BOLDLY CONCEIVED AND EXECUTED *Below*
This full-perspective elevation of the Robie House shows how the massed volumes work to create the building's unique sense of self-containment and permanence. It was a harbinger of the concepts embodied in the Broadacre City model constructed almost thirty years later.

THE COURTYARD RESIDENCE *Previous pages & opposite*
The expansive Avery Coonley House (pages 166-67) in parklike Riverside, Illinois, is a variation on the basic cruciform designs of the smaller Prairie houses. Its U-shaped plan (1908) loosely encloses a spacious court-yard, the entrance to which is pictured here. On the opposite page is the beautifully detailed Melvyn Maxwell Smith House in Bloomfield Hills, Michigan—an L-shaped Usonian courtyard-style dwelling designed in 1946 and enlarged by Taliesin Associated Architects.

A CROWN OF TRELLISWORK *Above*
The concrete-block façade of the Eric Pratt House in Galesburg, Michigan (1948), is shaded by slender tiers of red-stained mahogany that filter the light to its in-line rooms. This is one of the four Wright designs executed for the Country Home Acres development after World War II.

SOUTHWESTERN CULTURAL CENTER *Overleaf*
The Dallas Theater Center's Kalita Humphreys Theater (1955) is an almost windowless concrete-cantilever build-ing that reflects the hot Texas sun. Its focal point is the circular stage drum that rises above the roofline, housing a revolving stage that can also be raised and lowered.

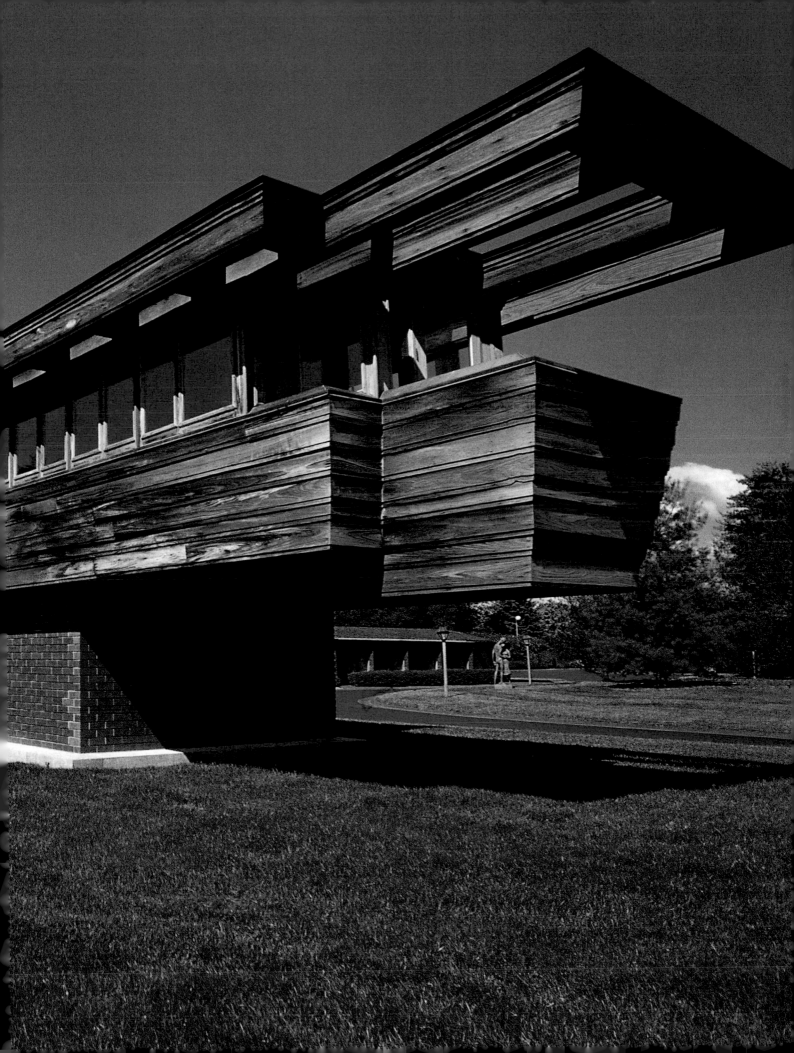

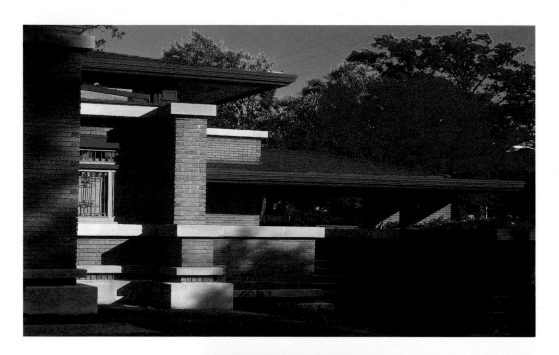

LIKE A SHIP AT SEA *Previous pages*
The cantilevered, cypress-clad master bedroom of the
Herbert F. Johnson House in Wind Point, Wisconsin,
thrusts far from its brick supports, emphasizing the sheer
size and power of this unique multilevel country house,
which is appropriately called Wingspread and occupies
a twenty-acre site (1937).

AN ORCHESTRAL COMPOSITION *Opposite and below*
The ageless Meyer May House (1908), in Grand Rapids,
Michigan, with its broad eaves, overhanging ornamental
latticework, and bountifully planted terraces that extend
seamlessly into the grounds, is a premier example of all
that Wright had sought—and realized—during the first
twenty years of his career.

INDOOR/OUTDOOR
GARDENS

Above: *The extensive grounds surrounding Wingspread, at Wind Point, Wisconsin, are meticulously maintained by the Johnson Foundation, which uses the estate as an administrative and conference center.*

Page 176: *Oriental influence pervades the courtyards and gardens at Taliesin, where Wright spent most of his life after leaving Oak Park in 1909. His widow, Olgivanna Wright, designed an enclosed memorial garden for him in 1959, the year of his death.*

One of Wright's largest commissions in the first phase of his career was that for the Avery Coonley House (1907) in Riverside, Illinois. As with the contemporaneous Robie House, he had a liberal budget to work with and a free hand in the design—one of his most elegant Prairie houses, on a beautiful site overlooking the Des Plaines River. The house has no excavated basement: the ground floor provides space for utilities and a large playroom that opens onto a terrace with an ornamental pool. The second (main) floor comprises a system of joined pavilions that overlook the lawns and gardens (both raised and sunken) from various heights. The flow of space from one living area to another is remarkably harmonious and commands vistas beyond the landscaped grounds—the "borrowed landscape" effect so prominent

in Oriental gardening. The community of Riverside was an idyllic setting, laid out by the pre-eminent landscape designer Frederick Law Olmsted, the co-creator of New York City's landmark Central Park.

According to William Allin Storrer, "Here a low Prairie house, Wright's first 'zoned plan,' is twice extended from central spaces….Wright places the main living room directly under the hip roof so that its ceiling partakes of the protective drooping overhang and attendant cave-like quality first achieved in the Heurtley house." A long corridor links this upper level with the bedroom wing. The estate included a gardener's cottage and a garage and stables (both 1911) and the unique Coonley Playhouse (actually a full-size kindergarten, or "cottage school," conducted by Mrs. Coonley, the heiress to the Ferry Seed Company fortune). This was a cruciform building centered on a stage and dressing room that faced the assembly room, with a scaled-down kitchen and workshop in the other two wings (1912). Perhaps its best-known feature is the triptych window series in Wright's "balloons and confetti" design. Replicas of the original twenty-two clerestory windows were installed in the late 1980s, while the original triptych windows have been removed to New York City's Metropolitan Museum of Art. The block-square property had ample room for all these structures, which at one period were divided among five different owners. Since then, the original residence has been fully restored and designated a National Historic Landmark.

The Coonley House remained one of Wright's favorites, and he recalled it in an article for a 1936 issue of London's *Architect's Journal*: "Freedom of floor space and the elimination of useless heights worked a miracle in the new dwelling place. A sense of appropriate freedom had changed its whole aspect."

Another type of project surfaced in 1913, when Wright's client and friend Edwin C. Waller, Jr., proposed a large-scale entertainment complex with an open-air restaurant just off Chicago's Midway. The city's sizeable German-American community would find this a familiar-style venue, comparable to a European-style beer garden, and Wright saw it as a year-round attraction, which would include a winter garden and an indoor ballroom and provide ample space for cultural as well as social events. Waller and his associates raised most of the $350,000 budget, and Wright quickly drew up the plans for Chicago's modernistic answer to the original Madison Square Garden designed by architect Stanford White for New York City.

Initial enthusiasm ran high, with sculptors Alfonso Ianelli and Richard Bock enlisted to execute sculptures and finials, while John Lloyd Wright, then twenty years old, painted murals and learned the supervisory skills he would need when he took charge of various projects of the 1920s in his father's absence. Engineer Paul Mueller, who had worked with Wright at Adler & Sullivan, served as general contractor. The multilevel, three-story complex of brick and patterned concrete took shape rapidly, ornamented with Bock's sculptures and Ianelli's "Sprites"—abstract female figures in geometric forms. They included a stylized nude holding a large sphere above her head and a figure holding two cubes that represented the square. The huge central courtyard had a stage at one end with an elaborate acoustic shell and was edged by plantings in large pedestaled urns. Tall pylons crowned by rectangular finials overlooked the courtyard from the massive indoor complex that housed the winter garden and the three-story restaurant.

However, the rapid construction schedule and financial pressures contributed to disagreements among the many creative temperaments involved—including Frank Lloyd Wright's. As he recalled later, "In the Midway Gardens...I tried to complete the synthesis: planting, furnishings, music, painting, and sculpture. But I found that musicians, painters, and sculptors were unable to rise to any such synthesis. Only in a grudging and dim way did most of them even understand it as an idea." The result was that the complex was barely finished before its grand opening, which featured performances by a well-known orchestra and renowned singers.

Right: This view of the terrace from the living room of the Gerald B. Tonkens House in Amberley Village, Ohio, shows the seamless interpenetration of indoor and outdoor spaces.

For several years, Midway Gardens flourished, but the accumulating burden of its debt—as with Madison Square Garden—outstripped income, and Waller lost the property. Under new ownership, attendance waned as the original atmosphere declined into that of a conventional beer garden. The advent of Prohibition in 1920 put an end to the project, which was finally razed in 1929, with very few remnants of its heyday preserved.

In 1917 a very fine Prairie house that has not received the attention it deserves was designed for Henry J. Allen in Wichita, Kansas. A distinguished journalist, he later became the governor of his state and served as an unofficial advisor to several presidents. The house he commissioned was a harbinger of the later Aline Barnsdall residence, often called the "Hollyhock House." The Allen House has an L-shaped plan, with a very large single-story living room whose windows are recessed between brick piers. They face onto the street side of the property and into a large outdoor living space including the terrace, pool, and garden. The two-story portion of the house contains family and guest rooms and a sleeping porch, all accessed by a long tunnel gallery, and located above the kitchen and garage.

Exterior planters along the main façade not only beautify the street-side view, but serve to buffer noise and emphasize the striking horizontal lines of the first-floor wing. The detached garden house at the end of the courtyard was renovated in 1971, and the entire property was restored by the Allen-Lambe House Foundtion after its purchase from Wichita State University.

Aline Barnsdall was the heiress to a fortune amassed by her father during the oil-drilling boom in Pennsylvania, which also made millionaires of the Rockefeller family. She was deeply involved in drama and the arts and had met Wright in Chicago during her teenage years. On a trip to Los Angeles — then a sparsely settled

Left: A sense of shelter was paramount in the Wright aesthetic, expressed here in a brick window bay where indoor plants and sculpture lead the eye to the winter garden beyond the Zimmerman House in Manchester, New Hampshire.

community—in 1919, she bought an olive orchard on the rise that she named Olive Hill and planned a complex to include her residence and two theaters to be designed by Wright, along with studios to house the artists and dramatists involved and several picturesque outbuildings. Some of these projects never came to fruition, but the Aline Barnsdall House soon became a local landmark.

The mansion was designed around a very large patio courtyard with lawns, pools, and fountains overlooked by low rooftops and terraces. The windows were small and recessed to minimize the sun's heat and glare. The exterior appears massive and closed, suggesting Mayan influence, and is ornamented with a band of stylized hollyhocks made of poured concrete, which Wright called art stone. This motif recurs in the column capitals and the art-glass window treatments.

It is clear that Wright was experimenting here with a new type of California house, very different from the Spanish Colonial and bungalow styles that prevailed in the region. The living room is very large, with an intricate skylight set over the ceiling-high fireplace surround, which has a reflecting pool at the hearth. Built-in seating that incorporates both lamps and tables extends diagonally from either side of the fireplace, and several free-standing chairs and hassocks that could double as seating complete the furnishings. A golden glow seems to encompass the room, from the sculptural modern ceiling to the Oriental screen illuminated from above by recessed lighting. The dining room furniture carries out the hollyhock motif in tall-backed chairs with a matching table that are markedly different from Wright's earlier dining sets.

The music room and library flank the living room and open to views of the expansive terrace and the square pool beyond it. A central loggia overlooks the long garden court, which terminates in a circular pool. This courtyard was sometimes used for theatrical performances in which spectators seated below watched actors and dancers on the rooftops and terraces. Several bedrooms and the nursery were designed to overlook a patio on one side of the house, while the kitchen, servants' quarters, and kennels occupied the other side. The original landscaping for this imposing house was designed by Lloyd Wright, but it was much altered in subsequent years. The architect's eldest son (whose gifts were often overshadowed by his famous parent's reputation) also oversaw restoration of the house (1974–76), which has long been owned by the city of Los Angeles.

The Wrights' Los Angeles office, opened in the early 1920s, created the innovative textile-block houses of this period, which are so ideally suited to southern California's climate and terrain. The first, and some critics say the most successful, was the Alice Madison Millard House (1923) in Pasadena. As mentioned earlier, Wright now took the humble, precast concrete block and refashioned it into a unique building material impressed with decorative patterns, or pierced to admit light. The concrete was poured into molds in which steel or wooden grids formed the designs on one or both sides, and the resulting patterned blocks were "woven together" with steel rods inserted into hollow grooves. Mrs. Millard, recently widowed, had lived in a Wright-designed house in Highland Park, Illinois, during her marriage and agreed readily to the site chosen and the proposed building plans.

Opposite: Trellised esplanades with planting beds below connect all of the Wright-designed buildings at Florida Southern College (1938) in Lakeland, which Wright called "a Child of the Sun."

"La Miniatura," as the cubic house was called, was located in a wooded ravine shaded by eucalyptus trees. It rose gracefully to a height of three stories, surrounded by multilevel terraces. The two-story living room has a mezzanine above the chimney breast and French doors that open to a cantilevered balcony. Segments of the block formations are pierced in a cross-shaped pattern to admit light, and the interpenetration of exterior and interior ornament formed by the patterned blocks marked a new synthesis in organic architecture. A reflecting pool captures the natural beauty of the house and its setting, which includes weeping willows and climbing vines that soften the exterior. Wright reflected in his autobiography that "I would rather have built this little house than St. Peter's in Rome."

A series of Los Angeles clients soon demanded their own textile-block houses, which took shape rapidly over the next few years. The handsome three-level house built for John Storer (1923) rises from a terrace supported by a wall of plain and patterned blocks overhung by trailing plants in built-in containers. One enters the central portion of the flat-roofed residence through French doors into the combined reception hall/dining room. A sequence of narrow windows between patterned columns rises to illuminate this area and the high-ceilinged living room on the top floor as well.

One wing houses family bedrooms and baths, the other, utility areas. A semidetached garage is accessed by a driveway around the second wing. Mature plantings on the hillside site contribute to the beauty of this essay in textile-block construction, which incorporates three types of blocks: patterned, pierced, and plain. Lloyd Wright was instrumental in seeing the house to completion, and it was fully renovated and restored during the 1980s by architects Joel Silver and Eric Wright, the grandson of Frank Lloyd Wright.

The Samuel Freeman House (1924) was commissioned by a successful jeweler and his wife, who was a dancer: both belonged to an artistic group that formed a close-knit community whose members entertained one another frequently. The house was ingeniously contrived to make the most of a small lot on a steep slope in the Hollywood foothills of Los Angeles. The concrete-block and glass façade commands a view of abundant natural vegetation and a careful selection of cultivated plants, while the interior plan overlooks a terrace ornamented with native plants. The primary construction materials include eucalyptus and fir painted to simulate redwood, which provide warm color to the two-story interior. The second (entry) level includes the living room, balcony, and garage, with private spaces housed on the lower level. The furniture was designed by R.M. Schindler, then a student of Lloyd Wright, who made the working drawings and designed the landscaping. When Mrs. Freeman died in 1986, the house passed to the University of Southern California by way of a living trust.

What is now the Ennis-Brown House, built on a spur of the Santa Monica Mountains overlooking Los Angeles, was designed in 1923 for Charles Ennis. The largest of the four California textile-block houses of this period, its massive linear façade is composed of plain and patterned blocks, and the floor space comprises some 3,000 square feet (280 square meters). The walls are tapered, and the large art-glass windows are deeply recessed and hooded, which gives the house a monumental

Mayan quality, to which the extended terraces contribute. Well-defined living areas, with richly textured concrete-block walls and columns, include the large living room, dining room, and family bedrooms. The impressive interior has served as a movie set for several films.

A notable feature is the art-glass mural used as a fireplace surround—the only one of three designed for installation in Wright residences that has survived. According to Thomas A. Heinz, "All had the same theme—a blooming wisteria vine, and all were nearly identical apart from differences in size. The pendant flowers were in shades of blue, pink and white, and the leaves were quite unusual in that they were cut and painted with a gold wash before refiring in an oven and allowed to cool slowly," which produced a crackled effect. The art-glass firm of Giannini & Hilgart made all three of these murals.

Left: *Abundantly planted raised beds and tropical trees beautify the entrance to the textile-block John Storer House in Hollywood (1923), restored during the 1980s by Joel Silver and third-generation architect Eric Wright.*

The house changed hands many times before it was purchased by Mr. and Mrs. August Brown in 1968. By then, it was in dire need of restoration, which the Browns carried out. They also founded the Trust for Preservation of Cultural Heritage to maintain it for the future—a contribution recognized in the change of name to the Ennis-Brown House.

The year of the stock-market crash that initiated the Great Depression brought Wright a welcome commission from his cousin Richard Lloyd Jones, a successful newspaper publisher in Tulsa, Oklahoma. Called Westhope, this large concrete-block house was considerably different from those designed for California. Constructed of alternating vertical members of plain concrete block and steel-framed glass, it appears taller than its two-story height. The roof is flat except at the end of either wing, where mitred-glass enclosures extend upward and outward to serve as conservatories for plants including full-grown trees. Elegant landscaping contributes to the indoor/outdoor garden effect. In a 1931 catalog for a European exhibition of his works, Wright described it as "The dwelling house without walls."

Early in the Usonian period, Wright designed a beautiful house for John C. Pew in Shorewood Hills, Wisconsin (1938). This is an elevated, cantilevered building sited on a hillside overlooking Lake Mendota. Full-height glass doors open to the living-room terrace with its view of the "wild garden" and the lake beyond it. Constructed of limestone and cypress, which has weathered to a silver-grey color, the house has a modest public façade, but ample living quarters on two stories that encompass 1,200 square feet (110 square meters). Bedrooms and a full bath are on the upper level. During the 1990s, the house was renovated by its second owners, Dr. John S. and Cynthia Edwards, who replaced the original wood-slat kitchen floor with flagstone and reconfigured the kitchen skylight to adhere more closely to Wright's original design for the transom level.

One of the last and most impressive Usonians is the John Rayward House (1955), in New Canaan, Connecticut. The largest Wright residence on the East Coast, it is graced with a set of circular pools and a grotto that merges with a natural stream on the scenic property. Called Tirranna, from the Australian aboriginal word for "running waters," it occupies a twenty-acre site and combines an elliptical living and dining area overlooking the planted terrace and an L-shaped addition with five bedrooms, including the master bedroom surmounted by an observatory above the dressing room. A Wright-designed playhouse for the Rayward's two daughters was added in 1957, and the second owner, Herman R. Shepherd, retained Taliesin Associated Architects to provide a major extension whereby the workspace was enlarged, the courtyard enclosed, and a greeenhouse and connecting pergola added. According to William Allin Storrer, the property was landscaped by Frank Okamura, landscape architect of the Brooklyn Botanical Garden, and Charles Middeleer. He adds that "The grounds contain such a quantity and variety of flora as to qualify as a major botanical garden." The plates that follow illustrate far-ranging examples of Wright's compelling ideal, "the House Beautiful," through various stages of his career.

Opposite: The atrium of California's Marin County Civic Center Administration Building (1957) affords a view of this indoor garden from the two upper levels.

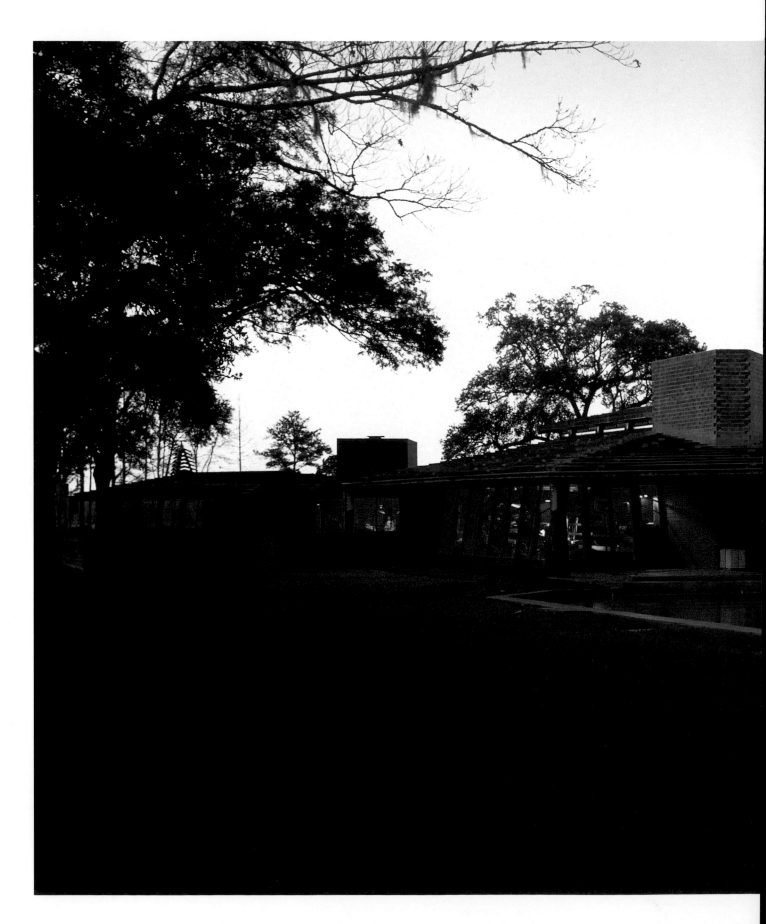

CONTEMPORARY PLANTATION   *Previous pages*

One of Wright's most unusual designs was that for the extensive Auldbrass Plantation in Yamassee, South Carolina (begun 1938). On pages 188–9 is the misty view from the Stevens House, where decorative downspouts (foreground) evoke the local Spanish moss. Pages 190–91 show the recently restored Pool House, with its inward-sloping walls of red brick, Tidewater cypress, and clear glass. Cypress is used throughout the complex to harmonize with the many live oaks on lowlands that were originally cultivated as a rice plantation.

SHIP-LAP CYPRESS SIDING   *Above*

Feathery plumes in the hillside garden of the Gregor S. Affleck House highlight the intricate fretwork windows of this Bloomfield Hills, Michigan, residence (1940), restored to its original beauty by the Lawrence Institute of Technology during the 1980s.

"SNOWFLAKE"   *Opposite*

The secluded C. David Wall House (1941) in Plymouth, Michigan, is named for its hipped roof with pierced overhanging trellises, which creates a snowflake form when viewed from above.

SHAPED FROM THE DESERT   *Pages 194-197*

Bold, sculptural forms create a shade-giving pergola at Taliesin West (1938) on the 600-acre Maricopa Mesa, near Scottsdale, Arizona (pages 194–5). On page 196, a stark metal sculpture emphasizes the low, triangular forms of the desert compound. The rubblestone bell tower (page 197), crowned by metal diagonals, summons members of the Taliesin Fellowship to meals three times a day.

TWO VIEWS OF THE TOWER *Opposite and below*
This dramatic leaning light tower, with its triangular buttress, supports the Cherokee–red square-within-a-square that served as Wright's logo when the tower was built in 1953. Thomas A. Heinz has called Taliesin West "the supreme definition of organic architecture."

A WOODWARD TERRACE *Overleaf*
The graceful curved terrace on the private façade of the Kenneth Laurent House (1949) in Rockford, Illinois, overlooks a long slope leading down to Spring Creek. On the following pages (202–03), the semicircular window wall of the Laurent House integrates the well-appointed living room with the wooded grounds framed by the wide arc of the eaves.

BRINGING THE OUTDOORS IN *Previous pages*

The enclosed terrace of the Isabel Roberts House in River Forest, Illinois, has been altered several times to accommodate the growth of the British elm tree that rises through the roof.

FINISHING TOUCHES *Overleaf*

Page 208: Integrated planters with cascades of foliage and a footed urn on a short pier enhance the façade of the G.C. Stockman House in Mason City, Iowa. On page 209, the spacious courtyard of the Aline Barnsdall House overlooking Los Angeles was the scene of lavish entertainments by its owner, a patroness of the arts who called the house her "California Romanza."

PRIVATE WORLDS *Opposite and above*

An openwork bench well sheltered by the eaves (above) affords a clear view of the manicured grounds of the Melvyn Maxwell Smith House in Bloomfield Hills, Michigan. On the opposite page is the shallow stepped terrace that invites one into the garden of the William Palmer residence in Ann Arbor, Michigan. ClayCraft of Columbus, Ohio, coordinated the masonry elements of this elegant 1950 house.

"MORE STATELY MANSIONS" *These pages and overleaf*
The south terrace of the exquisite Meyer May House (window detail above) is a study in the masterful combination of diverse materials to create an enclave that ascends by degrees from ground level to the topmost roofline.

Overleaf, the warm glow that emanates from the expansive window-walls of the Melvyn Maxwell Smith House in Bloomfield Hills, Michigan, illuminates the snow-covered winter garden with a beauty all its own.

THE GRAMMAR
OF SIMPLICITY

Page 214 and above:
The main sanctuary of
Beth Sholom Synagogue
located in Elkins Park,
Pennsylvania (1954),
centers on the beautiful
ark that contains the
Torah and the triangular
stained-glass chandelier
(detail above) that
symbolizes light and the
inexpressible attributes
of God. Jewish law prohibits
graphic representations
of the Divine as "graven
images."

"The beauty of the house resides first in its geometry, its adherence to basic principles of organic spatial design. With Wright, this was achieved through use of the unit system, which to this architect was as the staff and bar lines are to a musician."

This astute observation by William Allin Storrer helps us to understand the simplicity and order that are inherent in the Wright aesthetic. The many and varied geometric modules that he used throughout his long career share these underlying principles, whether they are expressed in the form of circles and arcs, cruciforms, hexagons, squares and rectangles, triangles, diamonds, spirals, or combinations thereof. These are, indeed, "the staff and bar lines" that carry out the orchestral theme of his seventy-year career—most of a lifetime dedicated to the passionate pursuit of his career. As Wright himself observed in *Sixty Years of Living Architecture* (1951):

"The song, the masterpiece, the edifice are a warm outpouring of the heart of man—human delight in life triumphant: we glimpse the infinite. That glimpse or vision is what makes art a matter of inner experience—therefore sacred, and no less but rather more individual in this age, I assure you, than ever before." It is doubtful that the quest for money, prestige, or ego satisfaction alone could have driven Wright to the ceaseless labor he imposed upon himself in the face of many disappointments, or to broaden public understanding of his ideas on an architecture relevant to a modern democratic society.

Hundreds of his unbuilt projects are preserved in the archives of the Frank Lloyd Wright Foundation, in beautiful renderings that round out the visionary quality of Wright's work, including, for example, the "Mile High Tower" proposed for Chicago in 1956. At the base of this needlelike steel spire—5,280 feet (1,609 meters) tall, with 528 floors—he sketched in, for scale, four monumental constructions that were dwarfed by the tower: the Washington Monument, the Pyramid of Cheops, the Eiffel Tower, and the Empire State Building (then the world's tallest building). His premise was that only a few such "Sky City" towers could replace the high-density skyscrapers that gave an inhuman scale to cities like Chicago and New York, thus providing large, open areas of green space and low-level shops and dwellings congruent with his concept of Broadacre City, with its motto "A New Freedom." However, as Robert McCarter points out in his chapter on the cantilevered tower in *Frank Lloyd Wright*: "Wright's Mile High Tower was destined from its inception never to be realized; not because it was technically unbuildable, for it was within that realm of possibility, but because Wright presented it as a purely abstract exercise, not conceiving it as he had his other high-rise designs as a place scaled to and ordered by human experience."

A random sampling of executed works illustrates how closely Wright conformed to the contours of a given site, the client's needs and interests, and the nature of the materials employed. He never swerved from his resolution that "Each building will have a grammar of its own, true to materials, as in the new grammar of Fallingwater, my first dwelling in reinforced concrete." Always he opted for the best quality, whether of wood, stone, metal, glass, textiles, brick, landscaping, or lighting. This made him notorious for his cost overruns, but the prosperous client was usually so gratified by the results that he swallowed hard and paid double or triple what he had planned to. In the case of enthusiastic young couples who were determined to have a Wright design even though it was beyond their means, he found ways to economize without compromising the quality of the work. Many of his Usonian houses were partially built by middle-income clients who did much of the work themselves, saving on contractors' fees as they learned to mix and pour cement, or to apply plywood veneers to interior walls.

Below: The soaring bell tower of the Annie Merner Pfeiffer Chapel at Florida Southern College (1938) has a breezeway-shaped skylight supported by triangular steel beams and commands a view of the entire campus.

Above: The cylindrical elevator shaft whose bright reflective surface illuminates a dark corner of the main building of the Johnson Wax Building (1939) located in Racine, Wisconsin.

As we have observed, Wright's own dwellings were a laboratory for his ideas, and he often went deeply into debt to perfect them, as at Taliesin, building and rebuilding. This house exemplifies his unique appreciation for stone as a building material, which "as human hands begin upon it—stonecraft—becomes a shapely block. The block is necessarily true to square and level, so that one block may securely rest upon another and great weight be carried to greater height"

(unpublished manuscript, 1937). In the same source, he expresses his love for wood, describing the living tree as "a flower of light" and concluding that "Wood is the most humanly intimate and of all materials the most kindly to man."

As early as 1890, Wright designed a summer cottage for his then employer, Louis H. Sullivan, in Ocean Springs, Mississippi, where a small resort community of people from Chicago had been established. The good-sized cottage was organized along the lines of a cross, with a plan that placed utilities and services in a back wing—a harbinger of the Prairie houses that would emerge more fully in the early 1900s. An unbuilt project for Edwin Waller in River Forest, Illinois (1898), was the first fully realized cruciform house, with a central entrance hall surrounded by four single-room wings: the entrance porch, living and dining rooms, and kitchen-stair (utility) area.

The handsome Edwin H. Cheney House (1903) in Oak Park is a single-story brick residence with a hipped roof, wide chimney, and a walled terrace that contributes to privacy without obtruding upon the lines of the house. The entrance hall opens on one side to the long, richly appointed living room with a banded ceiling and on the other to a corridor that separates the private spaces, including five bedrooms and several dressing rooms. The basement—a feature Wright would soon abandon in most of his residential architecture—housed storage and laundry rooms. Originally, the house was surrounded by gardens, with a fountain that had built-in stone benches.

Another Oak Park house was scaled down after the death of client Thomas Gale to suit the needs of his widow,

Laura, who wished to stay in the community on a smaller lot. The compact, modern house designed for her in 1909 differed from the Prairie style in having a flat roof and minimal eaves. Substantial piers crowned with urns rise from ground level to the second-story balcony. Inside, the living and dining areas are separated by stairs, and large doors open from the living room to the walled porch.

As Wright's practice extended beyond the Chicago area and its suburbs, new sites and climates challenged his creative mind. The Carroll Alsop House located in Oskaloosa, Iowa (1948), is an outstanding Usonian design on a large lakefront property. Intersecting roof angles above the spacious square living room focus the view toward the lake. The gentle, rolling slope of the site is defined by brick piers and planters that flank the stairs to the entry, and red brick with cypress are combined in the ceilings and window frames to striking effect.

In the Northwest, Wright designed an unusual house for lumber merchant Chauncey L. Griggs in the busy port of Tacoma, Washington (1946). It overlooks a stream that defines one edge of the property and is unusual in having a single-pitched peaked roof. The concrete-block construction is now wreathed with mature plantings that attest to the mild climate and fertile soil of the region, well known for its many abundant orchards, rose gardens, and rhododendrons.

The Raymond Carlson House, Phoenix, Arizona, designed for the editor of *Arizona Highways*, is well suited to its Southwest location, comprising a multilevel space shaded by wide overhangs and built on a square module that uses wooden posts painted sky blue spanned by insulated panels to moderate the sun's glare during daylight hours. The desert-style garden is primarily paved and pebbled, with planting beds inset to conserve water and large-scale decorative features including a smooth, rounded urn with a burnished silver/blue patina. The interior combines parquet floors, banded partitions, and a concrete-block chimney core with adjacent cushioned seating.

Below: The arcades of the skyway linking the Research tower and Administration building of the Johnson Wax Building illustrate his departure from conventional industrial design toward flowing organic shapes.

Above: *Wright's affinity for circular and spiral-shaped forms became more pronounced during the latter half of his career, as seen in the Curtis Meyer House at Galesburg, Michigan (1948).*

The Seymour Shavin House (1950) is the only Wright building in the state of Tennessee, built in Chattanooga on the Missionary Ridge of Civil War fame. Laid up in strong courses of stonework, it has a dramatic diagonal roofline over the glass-paned living area, which frames a view of the Tennessee River. The bedroom wing is a half-level below the common spaces on account of the topography. The primary construction materials are local sandstone and red Louisiana cypress, and extending features include an upper and lower terrace and a sizable carport.

Many people are unaware that Wright designed a house for Marilyn Monroe and playwright Arthur Miller on a site in Roxbury, Connecticut, in 1957. The elaborate plan centered on a large, circular common space designed for entertaining, with a glass dome inset with cascades of glass spheres. Apparently, Mr. Miller had envisioned a simpler, more homelike dwelling, and since the couple separated before construction began, the project was never realized.

The exhibit entitled "Sixty Years of Living Architecture" opened in Florence, Italy, and toured Europe before it came to New York City in 1953. There it was displayed in the Usonian Exhibition House on the future site of the Guggenheim Museum, in Manhattan's Upper East Side. It faced into a pavilion built of pipe scaffolding surfaced with layers of corrugated glass and paneling composed of cement and asbestos board. The house itself was a spacious, light-filled environment that included a rectangular living/dining area with a wide band of clerestory windows and a glazed wall facing the terrace, a large central workspace, and a gallery opening to the children's and master bedrooms. The house attracted favorable attention from its many visitors, and Wright intended that it be auctioned and relocated when the exhibition closed. However, complications arose that prevented this from happening; in the event, the house was disassembled and sold in parts, the proceeds to benefit the Frank Lloyd Wright Building Conservancy.

Space prevents a detailed overview of the countless details and decorative features that enriched Wright's work over the years. Many pieces of built-in and freestanding furniture have been acquired by museums; others remain in their original settings, and still others have disappeared or been purchased by private collectors. The distinctive spindled chairs and dining sets, breakfronts and lighting fixtures, carpets and pottery designs went through many variations, some of which are now available as reproductions licensed by the Frank Lloyd Wright Foundation. To give a single example, the early tall-backed chairs in the Oak Park Home/Studio would reappear in many forms: medium-backed spindled dining chairs, as used in the Willits House; living-room spindle-box chairs with both straight and cantilevered backs; medium- and tall-backed chairs with panel insets instead of spindles; a spindle-box recliner resembling the traditional Morris chair; and octagonal-backed chairs with six short legs. One can trace this process of evolution from the chairs designed for the Peter A. Beachy House in Oak Park (1906) to those for the Donald Lovness House in Stillwater, Minnesota (1955).

Materials, too, changed over time, from the early oak furnishings to a variety of other woods suitable to both machine- and hand-crafting. As Thomas A. Heinz points out: "Wright spent most of his last twenty years exploring the possibilities of using plywood in his furniture, as it has great tensile strength and can also be used with larger solid members as a stable structural membrane." Plywood also lent itself to the alternative furniture arrangements that Wright favored, including hexagonal tables that could be reconfigured in many ways and brightly cushioned hassocks that doubled as extra informal seating. The diversity, richness, and durability of these telling features and many others is highlighted in the plates that follow.

Left: *A view over the Melvyn Maxwell Smith House showing the simple geometry of the planes of its flat roof.*

ANGLES AND PLANES *Previous pages*

The bold lines and angular forms of the interior space and furnishings of the Usonian homes built for Herman T. Mossberg (page 222) at South Bend, Indiana (1948), and for William Palmer (page 223) in Ann Arbor, Michigan (1950), are softened by concealed lighting and the rich tones of polished wood.

A MILESTONE IN COMMERCIAL ARCHITECTURE *Left*

The streamlined S.C. Johnson & Son complex took form between 1936 and 1944, when the Research Tower (far left) was added to the headquarters commissioned by Herbert F. Johnson for his family's wax company. Located in Racine, Wisconsin, the Administration Building (at right) opened in 1939 to general acclaim for its coherent, fluid design and innovative, ample, well-lighted workspaces.

THE FORM/FUNCTION PARADIGM *Pages 226–27*

On page 226 is the unique two-story Usonian Automatic house designed for Dorothy Turkel of Detroit, Michigan (1955). This L-shaped structure incorporates several different concrete-block forms, predominantly square, to carry the house to its full height. Page 227 shows a detail of the entrance to the pyramidal Beth Sholom Synagogue (1954) in Elkins Park, Pennsylvania, designed to evoke Mount Sinai. The menorah motif on the steel tripod that ascends to the roofline recurs throughout the temple.

THE CAMPUS OF THE FUTURE *Pages 228–31*

The use of contrasting geometric forms for the futuristic Florida Southern College in Lakeland (pages 228–29) gives the complex a harmonious sense of unity in diversity. On pages 230–31 are details of the circular Grady Gammage Memorial Auditorium at Tempe's Arizona State University, including a portion of the 55-foot (16.8-meter) concrete colonnade and (facing page) the balcony, with its rhythmic arches upholding light globes.

POISED FOR FLIGHT *Above and opposite*

The steeply angled, prow-shaped roof of the sanctuary (detail above) at the Shorewood Hills, Wisconsin, Unitarian Church (1947) lends this long, low house of worship an aerodynamic look.

ECHOES OF BYZANTIUM *Pages 234–37*

The ground plan of the Annunciation Greek Orthodox Church in Wauwatosa, Wisconsin, is based on the pedestal-mounted emblem on page 234—an equal-armed Greek cross combined with a circle. The detail on page 235 shows the curved entryway sheltered by the bowl-shaped balcony above it, raised on one of the four great concrete piers. The full-façade view on pages 236–7 illustrates how this remarkable house of worship merges the primary symbols of the Greek Orthodox faith: the dome and the cross.

ART-STONE ORNAMENT *Above*

The monolithic exterior of the Aline Barnsdall House overlooking Los Angeles is studded with stylized hollyhocks of cast concrete tinted gold by adding crushed granite from the site. This abstract motif infuses the design of the whole complex.

MASTERFUL BRICKWORK *Below*

The arched entryway to the Arthur Heurtley House in Oak Park (1902) is sheltered by a low wall of matching Roman brick pierced by apertures to create patterns of light. The entire façade comprises horizontal courses of brick that project at intervals to suggest board-and-batten siding. This detail of one of Wright's favorite houses exemplifies what he called "elimination of the insignificant."

BUILDINGS FOR "BROADACRE CITY" *Pages 240–43*

Pages 240 & 241: Two views of the intricate aluminum pylon designed to serve both as a ventilation tower and radio antenna at the Marin County Civic Center Administration Building (1957) in San Rafael, California. On page 242, semicircular signs identify the various government offices in the Civic Center, which includes the Hall of Justice and the Marin County Post Office, both completed after Wright's death by Taliesin Associated Architects. Continuous angled arcades form a breezeway at Florida Southern College in Lakeland (page 243).

234

COUNTY RECORDER

TRANSLUCENT TAPESTRIES *These pages and overleaf*

Squares and rectangles are interwoven to form prisms of light in the clerestory and the coffered ceiling of Oak Park's Unity Temple (opposite and below). On page 246, tall, narrow art-glass windows in the living room of Milwaukee's F.C. Bogk House (1916) are deeply recessed to provide privacy on a narrow city lot. The landing of the E.E. Boynton House in Rochester, New York (1908, page 247), is illuminated by vertical panels that lead the eye to the second-floor ceiling level.

ADVENTURES IN WORKSPACE *Pages 248–51*

The photograph on pages 248–49 shows the comfortable, top-lighted cafeteria in the Johnson Wax Company headquarters in Racine, Wisconsin, which has streamlined furniture designed by Wright, as do all the office spaces throughout the building. The advertising department's impressive reception area in the Johnson Research Tower (shown on pages 250–51) features a magnificent domed ceiling of Pyrex tubing spangled with circles of varying sizes.

GLOSSARY

The following brief definitions cover architectural terms used in this book.

BALUSTER A row of miniature columns or spindles supporting a stair rail or used to form decorative screens, etc.

BATTEN A narrow strip of wood used between boards, as for siding, to prevent warping

BREAKFRONT A sideboard or cabinet with a projecting central section

BUTTRESS Masonry pier used to reinforce walls

CAMING Metal framework for an art-glass window or panel, usually made of lead

CANTILEVER A projecting beam, balcony, or other structure supported at only one end

CAPITAL The top part, or head, of a pillar or column

CASEMENT WINDOW A narrow window with sashes that open outward on hinges

CLERESTORY A series of windows high in a wall, or rising into a separate story

COFFER A decorative sunken panel, as in a ceiling, vault, or dome

COLONNADE A row of columns connected at the top in the Classical manner

COPING The top layer of a masonry wall that protects it from water damage

EAVES The lower edge of a roof, usually projecting beyond the sides of a building

ELEVATION A flat scale drawing of the front, rear, or side of a building

FANLIGHT A half-circle window, often with sash bars arranged like the ribs of a fan

FRAME The supporting structure, or skeleton, of a building

FRETWORK Ornamental three-dimensional geometric designs or other symmetrical figures (frets) enclosed in a band or border

FRIEZE Decorative band around a wall

GYPSUM PLASTER Incorporates a type of chalk (gypsum) found in sedimentary rocks; also called plaster of Paris

HIP The angle formed by the meeting of two adjacent sloping sides of a roof

INGLENOOK A recessed area containing a fireplace with built-in seating on either side

ICONOSTASIS An openwork screen decorated with icons that separates the sanctuary of an Eastern Orthodox church from the rest of the interior

INLAID Decorated with veneers of fine materials set into the surface

LOAD-BEARING Capable of carrying a load in addition to its own weight, as in a load-bearing wall

MITRED-GLASS WINDOWS Corner windows without supports or divisions

MULLION A vertical window division

PEDESTAL URN A wide, shallow urn on a footed base, often used as a planter

PIER Supporting post or stone, often square, thicker and shorter than a column

PORTE-COCHERE A roof projecting over a driveway at the entrance to a building

PORTICO Colonnaded entry porch

SIDING Boards, shingles, or other material used to surface a frame building

SOFFIT The underside of a structural component—eaves, beams, arches, etc.

STRINGCOURSES Wooden moldings used to define sections of a wall or ceiling

STUCCO A durable finish for exterior walls, applied wet and usually composed of cement, sand, and lime

TAPESTRY BRICK Colored brick interspersed with light-tan brick

TERRA COTTA A hard, semifired ceramic clay used in pottery and building construction

BIBLIOGRAPHY

Bernstein, Fred A. "Renovating Frank Lloyd (W)right," *Metropolitan Home*, Nov/Dec 1997.

_____. "Meeting Mr. Wright," *Metropolitan Home*, Feb 1992.

De Long, David G., ed. *Frank Lloyd Wright: Designs for an American Landscape, 1922–1932*. N.Y.: Harry N. Abrams, in assoc. with the Canadian Centre for Architecture, the Library of Congress, & The Frank Lloyd Wright Fdn., 1996.

Heinz, Thomas A. *The Vision of Frank Lloyd Wright*. Edison, N.J.: Chartwell Books, 2000.

Hollingsworth, Mary. *Architecture of the 20th Century*. London: Brompton Books, 1988.

Hoppen, Donald W. *The Seven Ages of Frank Lloyd Wright: A New Appraisal*. N.Y.: Capra Press, 1993.

Johnson, Samuel C. "Mr. Wright and the Johnsons of Racine, Wisconsin," *AIA Journal*, Jan 1979.

Kreisman, Lawrence. "Prairie Meets the Sound," *The Seattle Times*, Feb 20, 2000.

McCarter, Robert. *Frank Lloyd Wright*. London: Phaidon Press, 1997.

Pfeiffer, Bruce Brooks. *Frank Lloyd Wright Drawings*. N.Y.: Harry N. Abrams, in assoc. with The Frank Lloyd Wright Fdn. & the Phoenix Art Museum, 1990.

_____ and Gerald Wordland, eds. *Frank Lloyd Wright: In the Realm of Ideas*. Carbondale: So. Ill. Univ. Press, in assoc. with The Frank Lloyd Wright Fdn., 1988.

Storrer, William Allin. *The Architecture of Frank Lloyd Wright: A Complete Catalog*, 2nd ed. Cambridge, Mass.: The MIT Press, 1978.

Tafuri, Manfredo, and Francesco Dal Co. *Modern Architecture*. N.Y.: Harry N. Abrams, 1979.

Wright, Frank Lloyd. "In the Cause of Architecture," *Architectural Record* 23, Mar 1908.

_____. *Two Lectures on Architecture*. Chicago: Art Institute of Chicago, 1930.

_____. *An Autobiography*, 3rd ed. (rev.). N.Y.: Duell, Sloan and Pearce, 1943.

_____. *The Story of the Tower*. N.Y.: Horizon Press, 1956.

INDEX

ACKNOWLEDGMENTS AND PHOTO CREDITS

The publisher would like to thank the following individuals and organizations for their assistance in the preparation of this book: Sara Hunt, editor; Simon Ethan Saunders, photo editor; Nikki L. Fesak, graphic designer/art director; Erin Pikor, for the front jacket design; Lisa Langone Desautels, indexer; Robin Langley Sommer; Monica Korab; Elaine Rocheleau; Charles J. Ziga; the Johnson Wax Company; and the owners and representatives of each of the buildings featured in this book. Photographs of Fallingwater used with permission of Western Pennsylvania Conservancy. Fallingwater is located in Mill Run, Pennsylvania, telephone (724) 329 8501. All photographs of the Dana-Thomas House are reproduced by courtesy of the Illinois Historic Preservation Agency.

The publisher also gratefully acknowledges the photographers for permission to reproduce their copyright images, which appear on the pages listed:

© **Balthazar Korab:** 1, 3, 6, 9, 10, 12, 18, 19, 22, 24, 25, 26, 27, 28, 29, 30, 32, 33, 34, 35, 36, 37, 38, 39, 40, 41, 42, 43, 44, 45, 48, 49, 50, 51, 52, 57, 66, 68, 69, 70, 82, 86, 87. 102, 106, 107, 110, 111, 114, 116, 120, 121, 127, 134, 135, 136, 137, 138, 139, 143, 144, 145, 147, 148, 149, 150, 151, 152, 154, 155, 158, 160, 161, 162, 164, 166, 168, 169, 170, 174, 175, 182. 185. 187. 192, 193, 194, 196, 197, 198, 199, 206, 208, 209, 211, 212, 216, 217, 220, 221, 222, 226, 227, 228, 230, 231, 234, 235, 236, 238, 240, 241, 242, 243, 244, 245; © **Christian Korab:** 98, 122, 123; 176, 204, 239, endpapers; © **Paul Rocheleau:** 2, 15, 16, 21, 31, 38, 39, 41, 46, 54, 58, 60, 61, 62, 64, 72, 74, 75, 76, 78, 79, 80, 83, 84, 85, 88, 89, 90, 91, 92, 93, 94, 95, 96, 97, 99, 100, 104, 105, 108, 109, 112, 113, 117, 118, 124, 126, 128, 130, 132, 133, 156, 180, 181, 188, 190, 200, 202, 207, 210, 214, 218, 219. 223, 224, 232, 233, 246, 247, 248, 250; © **Charles J. Ziga:** 140, 142, 172, 178.